MAUI COOKS

ILLUSTRATIONS BY DARRELL ORWIG • NARRATIVE BY KAUI GORING
GRAPHIC DESIGN BY JILL WEED • RECIPES BY MAUI COOKS INC.

MAUI COOKS is a collection of treasured old recipes and contemporary Island tastes, reflecting the gracious style, informal charm and warm Aloha that has made Maui such a special place. It is "island style," mixing what is locally available and borrowing from the taste and techniques of the many ethnic cultures that make up Hawaii.

Published by Editions Limited, 1123 Kapahulu Avenue,
Honolulu, Hawaii 96816.

First Printing 1984
Printed in Singapore

Maui Cooks, Inc., 461 Aulii Drive, Pukalani, Maui, HI 96788

ISBN 0-915013-00-2

Typesetting by Ace Printing, Wailuku, Maui, Hawaii.
Cover Art by Darrell Orwig. Illustrations by Darrell Orwig.
Graphic Design by Jill Richards Weed.

CONTENTS

DEDICATION

We dedicate this book to Kokua Services, and these recipes to our friends, to Maui, and to those who generously contributed time and talent to the book. It is also dedicated to the pastry chefs who never got their just desserts, and the cooks whose names are on the tips of our tongues. Laughter and joy went into this book. We can hardly wait to share it.

WAIHEE COUNTRY STORE

It's easy to drive right past the Waihee Country Store, formerly the Fukunaga, without even a second thought. Its freshly stained red-brown front seems to blend perfectly with the trees and homes along the main road through the laconic, slightly-off-the-beaten-path town of Waihee. Once a bustling plantation town of Japanese, Filipinos, Portuguese, Hawaiians and an occasional "haole," the then Fukunaga Store was there for more than mere convenience. The small community depended upon it for groceries and liquor. Hanako Fukunaga remembers selling kerosene to her neighbors from the greasy, neglected drum sitting out front for their water heaters and cooking stoves. The town has not really changed much since those days. People have moved out and it is smaller, but the sleepy laziness remains. Today the store stocks more snacks, soda water and beer. Children ride up leaving their bikes on the wooden sidewalk for yellow and red balls of hard candy or bright pink chewing gum. Inside the floors are still the original wood planks. There are empty plastic yellow Pepsi cases off in one corner and two coolers are filled with beer, while a third holds carbonated soft drinks waiting for tourists in rental cars "going the other way" around Kahakuloa. Hanako Fukunaga says she misses the companionship she had when she was running the store, but these days she's just a few doors down the street working in her yard. She's not hard to miss.

CHICKEN LIVER PATE

2 tablespoons butter
1 teaspoon oil
1¼ pound chicken livers
1 medium onion, minced
2 large cloves garlic, crushed
1 teaspoon rosemary

2 teaspoons thyme
2 tablespoons parsley
1 cup butter, at room temperature
Dashes of nutmeg, salt and pepper
½ cup pistachios
½ cup clarified butter

Melt 2 tablespoons of butter with 1 teaspoon of oil in a skillet and saute the chicken livers, onion, garlic and rosemary until the livers are just barely cooked through, about 3 minutes. Put into a blender or food processor, add herbs and process until the mixture is smooth. Add 1 cup butter and mix again. Stir in nuts and pour into a serving bowl. Top with the clarified butter. Chill thoroughly before serving.

SPICY CREAM CHEESE

1 18-ounce jar pineapple preserves
1 18-ounce jar apple jelly
3 tablespoons dry mustard
⅓ cup horseradish

1 tablespoon cracked pepper
2 8-ounce packages cream cheese
Wheat Thins

Combine all ingredients except cream cheese and crackers and refrigerate. Soften cream cheese slightly. Shape into a pleasing form and refrigerate. When ready to serve, spread sauce over the cream cheese and surround with Wheat Thins.

CURRIED SHRIMP

2 to 3 pounds shrimp
2 tablespoons butter
2 tablespoons flour
2 cloves garlic
⅔ cup minced onion

⅔ cup minced apple
2 cups chopped fresh tomatoes
4 tablespoons curry, or to taste
3 cups mayonnaise
2 tablespoons lemon juice

Clean and peel shrimp. Put shrimp in boiling water for 2 to 3 minutes—just until pink—do not overcook. Drain and chill. Melt butter in a saucepan, add flour and mix thoroughly, then add garlic, minced onion, apple, tomatoes and curry. Stir over medium heat stirring constantly for about 3 minutes. Remove from heat and let cool. When thoroughly cool, add mayonnaise, shrimp and lemon juice. Refrigerate for several hours or overnight. Arrange on a plate or in a shallow bowl and serve with toothpicks.

ARTICHOKE CAVIAR

1 14-ounce can unmarinated
   artichokes
2 hard boiled eggs, grated

1 2-ounce jar black caviar
Mayonnaise

Drain and squeeze artichokes dry; then chop very fine. Line a small bowl with plastic wrap and layer as follows: ½ of the artichokes, a layer of mayonnaise, ½ of the grated egg, ½ of the caviar. Pack each layer down firmly. Repeat layers. Chill 2-3 hours. Turn out onto a bed of lettuce and serve with crackers.

COLD GINGER CHICKEN

½ cup fresh grated ginger
4 cloves garlic, grated
1 teaspoon Hawaiian salt or
   rock salt
1 cup oil

4 minced green onions
3 whole boneless chicken breasts
Bowl of ice water
Watercress for garnish

Mix ginger, garlic, salt, green onions and oil together until well blended. Cover and refrigerate at least 2 hours. Boil chicken breasts gently until just barely cooked, about 10 minutes. Remove from heat and plunge into ice water. Skin chicken, cover with plastic wrap and chill. When cold, cut chicken into 2″ pieces. Arrange nicely on a bed of watercress, leaving a space in the center of the plate for a bowl of sauce. Just before serving, pour sauce in a bowl and put on the plate with the chicken. We like to use chop sticks to dip the chicken pieces in the sauce, as it is quite thin.

BLUEWATER LAVISH ROLLS

1 pound cream cheese
4 cloves of garlic, finely chopped
5 middle eastern lavish (not to be confused with lavosh. Lavish is a middle eastern oval and pliable thin bread. Sometimes called Thin Thin. If unavailable use fresh flour tortillas.)

½ poung thinly sliced roast beef
1 tomato, cut into 5 slices
1 red Bermuda onion, finely chopped
10 watercress sprigs

Three days before serving blend cream cheese with the chopped garlic. Store in the refrigerator. At least 6 hours ahead of time, bring cheese to room temperature. Place lavish between damp towels to soften. Spread each lavish thickly with 1/5th of the cheese mixture. Lay 1/5th of the roast beef on the cream cheese. Sprinkle with 1/5th of the onion. See each tomato slice and open up to form a strip. Lay tomato and watercress sprigs on one edge of the lavish. Starting at that edge, roll lavish as tightly as possible. Wrap rolls in plastic wrap and chill for 4-5 hours. Cut off ends and slice into ¾" slices. The vegetables will be in the center of each slice. Spear with a toothpick and serve. This delicious recipe is from Bluewater Cuisine Catering of Kona, Hawaii.

PEPPERS AND BLUE CHEESE

6 bell peppers
6-8 cloves garlic, minced
¼ cup olive oil
1 tablespoon lemon juice or vinegar

Freshly ground pepper
Buttered biscuits, crackers or
    toast rounds
4 ounces blue cheese

Roast whole peppers by placing on a cookie sheet and broiling close to the flame, turning frequently, until all the skin has blistered and blackened. Remove from the oven and put in a plastic bag, or a brown paper bag or a damp towel, wrapping tightly. When the peppers are cool enough to handle, remove skins, seeds and membranes. Cut into eights and add enough olive oil to moisten thoroughly. Mix in garlic, and sprinkle with lemon juice or vinegar and freshly ground pepper, and marinate at least overnight. To serve, spread buttered biscuit, cracker or toast with blue cheese and then lay one or two strips of pepper on top. This unusual combination is very good served as a pupu, a snack or as part of a cold luncheon.

POISSON CRU

1 pound firm-fleshed white fish
  (ono, mahi mahi, ahi)
1 cup fresh lime or lemon juice
1 teaspoon salt
½ large round onion, finely chopped
4 stalks green onion, finely chopped
½ large green pepper, finely chopped
¾ cup finely chopped radishes
1 medium tomato, finely chopped
2-3 cloves of garlic, finely chopped
1 12-ounce can frozen coconut milk
Salt and pepper to taste

Cut fish into ½" cubes and marinate in lemon or lime juice and salt until "cooked," approximately 2-3 hours, depending on the size of the fish cubes. Drain and squeeze juice out of fish with cheesecloth or hands. Mix fish with vegetables, garlic and coconut milk and season with salt and pepper. Serves 8. This Polynesian dish is excellent as a pupu or first course. It is drippy, so serve it in small individual bowls or on salad plates on a bed of lettuce.

PUMPKIN SEEDS

1 6-ounce package of pumpkin seeds shelled
1 tablespoon shoyu, or to taste

Heat frying pan until quite hot. Put seeds in pan and stir and shake until seeds stop making a crackling sound. Transfer seeds to a bowl and sprinkle on just enough shoyu to flavor them. This is an absolutely delicious and healthy snack for children after school or for adults at cocktail time.

MORAGA MUSHROOMS

1 dozen large fresh mushrooms
6-8 slices bacon
1 3-ounce package cream cheese

Let the cream cheese come to room temperature. Remove stems from the mushrooms and discard. Wipe the caps and set aside. Fry bacon until crisp, drain on absorbent paper and chop into small pieces. Mix bacon pieces into cream cheese and divide among the 12 mushroom caps. Put stuffed caps on a cookie sheet and bake at 300 degrees for 10 to 15 minutes. Serve immediately.

KOKADA

1½ pounds fresh white ocean fish (ulua, ahi)
Lime juice to cover
1 12-ounce can frozen coconut milk
1 green onion, chopped
1 medium onion, grated
1 Hawaiian chili, seeded and chopped
Salt
Lemon slices
Tomato wedges

Remove skin and bones from fish and cut into ½" cubes. Place fish in a bowl and cover with lime juice. Marinate 2 hours. Combine coconut milk, grated onions, green onion and chopped chili. Drain fish and press out excess lime juice. Pour coconut mixture over fish and season to taste with salt. Serve as a pupu with toothpicks or as an appetizer with a slice of lemon and a wedge of tomato.

LOMI SALMON IN CHERRY TOMATOES

60 cherry tomatoes
¼ pound salted salmon*
3 green onion, thinly sliced
½ small Kula onion, finely chopped

Soak salmon in enough water to cover it for about 3 hours. Drain. Remove skin and bones. Shred salmon with two forks or fingers or in food processor. Combine with both onions and mix well. Set aside. Scoop out insides of cherry tomatoes and add to salmon mixture. Drain the tomato shells. Fill with salmon mixture and serve on a platter lined with ti leaves or any attractive fresh leaves. Serves 20.

*If salt salmon is not available you can use fresh and salt it well.

ABURAGE WITH FISHCAKE

3 cloves garlic, crushed and
  chopped
1 tablespoon sesame oil
3 tablespoons finely chopped onion
1 medium carrot cut into slivers
½-¾ cup string beans, cut in
  thin diagonal slices
½-¾ cup dried black mushrooms,
  soaked in water until soft,
  squeezed dry and finely chopped
2 tablespoons chopped parsley

1 tablespoon oyster sauce
1 pound Chinese fish cake mix
¼ cup finely chopped green onions
½ 5-ounce can water chestnuts,
  finely chopped
3 packages small aburage,
  (8 pieces per package), each
  piece cut in half diagonally
Pinch of red Hawaiian salt

Saute garlic in sesame oil about 1 minute. Add onion, carrots, mushrooms, beans, 1 tablespoon parsley and oyster sauce. Saute until vegetables are tender. Mix fish cake with chestnuts, 1 tablespoon parsley, green onion and a pinch of salt. Then mix in sauteed vegetables. Stuff each triangle of aburage with about 3 tablespoons of the filling. If you like, a peeled and deveined shrimp can be pushed down into the middle. Steam about 20 minutes. May be served with chili pepper sauce. (Don't be put off by this complicated-sounding recipe. Aburage is the familiar fried tofu used for cone sushi. Chinese fish cake mix is ground raw fresh fish readily available in packages in our supermarkets. This goes together quite easily and is a truly delicious and different pupu.)

CHILI PEPPER SAUCE

1½ cups shoyu
1½ cups rice vinegar
20 whole green to orange
   (under ripe) Hawaiian chili peppers

4-5 whole peeled garlic cloves
1 slice of ginger

Combine all ingredients in a jar and let age in the refrigerator – preferably for 2 weeks.

"MAVIS, MY LOVE" SOUP

8 peppercorns
2 bay leaves
3 cloves
3 large onions, coarsely chopped
½ cup butter
6 cups water

2 teaspoons salt
3 pounds potatoes, peeled and
  diced
½ pound Gruyere cheese, grated
1 egg, beaten
1 cup milk

Using a small piece of cheese cloth, tie the peppercorns, bay leaves and cloves into a bouquet garni. Cook onions in butter until limp. Add water, salt, potatoes and bouquet garni. Boil until potatoes are tender. Just before serving, blend the egg and cheese into the milk and add to the soup. Heat and stir until the cheese is melted. Delicious served with black bread.

JOOK

1 turkey carcass
1 package turkey wings
2 ribs celery
1 chung choi,* soaked in water,
  drained and chopped fine
1 small piece ginger, finely chopped

¼ cup chopped green onion
¾ cup rice (brown or white)
3 quarts water (or enough to cover
  carcass and parts)
1 head lettuce, chopped, for garni
Salt

Remove any meat left on turkey, cut up and set aside. Put turkey and the uncooked wings in large pot and cover with water. Add celery, chung choi and ginger. Simmer for at least 2 hours. Strain stock and discard all solids. Add reserved turkey meat, green onions and rice to the stock and continue to cook for 30 minutes, or until rice is cooked. Salt to taste. Put chopped lettuce in bowls and fill with hot soup. This is a particularly "Island" soup. What makes it unusually rich and delicious is the use of the turkey carcass with the flavor of the pork hash** stuffing inside. However, if you do not use a turkey that has been stuffed with pork hash, use up to ½ cup chung choi and ½ cup green onion. Chicken may be substitued for turkey.

*Chung choi is a salted cabbage found in packages in the Oriental section
  of the market.

**See index for pork hash recipe.

JANE'S HEARTY SOUP

4 ounces Portuguese sausage,
  sliced and/or
4 slices bacon
1 cup chopped onion
½ cup chopped celery
2 cloves garlic, minced
1 teaspoon basil
1 10½-ounce can beef bouillon

1 10½-ounce can bean with
  bacon soup
2 cups water
1 28-ounce can solid pack tomatoes
½ cup macaroni
1 cup shredded cabbage
1 cup sliced zucchini

Put all the ingredients except the macaroni into a large saucepan. Bring to a boil and simmer for at least a half an hour. While soup is simmering, cook the macaroni as directed on the package. Add to soup just before you are ready to serve.

WATERCRESS SOUP

3 pounds lean pork butt or
  pork scraps
Enough water to cover the pork
Salt and pepper to taste

2-3 eggs, beaten with a little
  cold water
1 large bunch of watercress,
  cut into 1" pieces

Put pork in a large soup pot. Cover meat with water. Cover the pot and simmer 2-3 hours, occasionally skimming off foam that will accumulate on the surface, until you have a rich broth and the pork is very tender. Remove pork from the pot, skim off fat and season the broth to taste with salt and pepper. Bring the broth back to a simmer and add the watercress. Stir and cook only long enough to slightly soften the stems. Slowly add the egg mixture in a steady stream, stirring constantly. Let cook 1-2 minutes until the egg is set. Serve immediately. This soup is unusual because it uses pork broth as a base. The result is a very rich, flavorful soup, and some cooked pork to use in other dishes.

BASIL WALNUT GARLIC SOUP

1 cup firmly packed fresh
    basil leaves
½ cup olive oil
½ cup walnuts

½ cup grated Parmesan cheese
3 large cloves garlic
8 cups chicken stock, heated

Blend first five ingredients in blender until thick and smooth. Add to hot stock and heat until very hot. Serve with additional Parmesan cheese sprinkled on top, if desired. This is a good way to use up all that extra basil! The soup has a lovely color, is light and delicious, and makes a wonderful first course.

GARLIC SOUP

6 tablespoons unsalted butter
2 leeks, chopped (about 2 cups)
¾ cup whole garlic cloves, peeled
6 cups chicken stock
6 cups potatoes, peeled and cubed
1½ cups heavy cream
2 cups homemade croutons
1 teaspoon salt

Melt half of the butter in a heavy saucepan and add the leeks and whole garlic. Steam on medium heat for 2 to 3 minutes. Add the stock and salt and bring to a boil. Cover and simmer for 45 minutes. Boil potatoes separately until just tender. Remove the leeks and the garlic from the stock and put in the blender. Drain the potatoes, but save the water, adding the potatoes to the leeks and garlic in the blender. Puree. Measure stock, adding some potato water if necessary to total 7 cups. Return pureed vegetables to the stock, add cream and heat to a boil. Swirl in the remaining butter and serve topped with croutons.

CURRIED BROCCOLI SOUP

2 pounds broccoli
2 14-ounce cans chicken broth
3 tablespoons butter or margarine
2 medium size onions, chopped

1½ teaspoon curry powder
Sour cream
Chopped salted peanuts

Trim tough stem ends from the broccoli. Cut off florets in bite-size pieces. Coarsely chop stems. Bring 1 cup of broth to a boil in a 3-quart saucepan. Add half of the florets and boil, uncovered, 3-4 minutes, or until just tender. Drain, saving the broth. Cover and chill florets to use as a garnish. In your original 3-quart saucepan melt the butter over medium heat; add the onion and the curry powder. Cook until the onion is limp. Stir in broccoli stems, remaining florets and the broth that you have saved. Cover and simmer until the vegetables are tender, about 12 minutes. Puree in batches in either a blender or food processor. Cover and chill. To serve, ladle into bowls. Top with reserved florets, sour cream and chopped peanuts. This is a year-round soup – wonderful cold, but also very good steaming hot.

EGGPLANT SOUP

1 medium onion, chopped
2 tablespoons olive oil
2 tablespoons butter
1 pound ground beef
1 large eggplant, peeled and diced
1 clove garlic, crushed
1 cup chopped carrots
1 cup diced celery
6-8 tomatoes, peeled and diced

3½ cups beef broth
½ teaspoon nutmeg
1 teaspoon sugar
1 teaspoon salt
½ teaspoon pepper
½ cup barley
2 tablespoons minced parsley
2 cups grated sharp Cheddar cheese

Saute onion in oil and butter until golden. Add meat and brown. Pour off excess fat from hamburger. Add eggplant, garlic, carrots, celery, tomatoes, broth, nutmeg, sugar, salt and pepper. Cover, reduce heat and simmer for 45 minutes. Add barley and parsley. Simmer 10 more minutes, or until the barley is cooked. Serve in big bowls, topped with grated cheese. This is a hearty soup which has never failed to elicit words of praise even from those who insist they hate eggplant!

PORTUGUESE BEAN SOUP

Bones from a roast beef
2-3 pounds lean round or stew beef,
  roasted about 30 minutes at
  400 degrees in the oven and
  then cut up
½ teaspoon garlic salt
4 stalks celery, including leaves
1 Kula onion, cubed
2 bay leaves
4 sprigs parsley
4 garlic cloves, unpeeled and
  slightly crushed
2 15-ounce cans kidney beans

1 28-ounce can whole tomatoes
2 carrots, peeled and cut in chunks
½ head cabbage, sliced
2 Kula onions, peeled and sliced
6 potatoes, peeled and cut in cubes
2 Portuguese sausages, sliced in
  discs and slightly sauteed
2 cups leftover roast beef or ham
½ teaspoon anise
¼ teaspoon each cinnamon, cloves,
  pepper
Salt to taste

Cover bones and meat with water. Add celery, onion, bay leaves, parsley and garlic cloves and simmer at least 4 hours. When stock is ready, strain and discard solid ingredients. Add the remaining ingredients to the stock and cook for at least 1½ hours longer.

CARROT GINGER SOUP

¾ cup minced onion
¼ cup peeled and minced ginger root
2 tablespoons oil
5 cups chicken stock
1½ pounds carrots, sliced
1½ cups half-and-half (light cream)

3 tablespoons unsalted butter
¼ cup flour
½ teaspoon cinnamon
Salt and pepper to taste
Fine julienne strips of carrots and
    ginger for garnish

Saute onion and ginger root in oil until onion is limp. Add stock and carrots, bring to a boil, cover and simmer for 35 minutes, or until the carrots are tender. Puree in the blender. Stir in half-and-half, return mixture to the saucepan and heat over low heat, stirring occasionally for 4 minutes. In a large saucepan melt butter, add flour and cook the roux until it is foamy, about 4 minutes. Stir carrot mixture into roux with cinnamon, salt and pepper. Simmer soup 5 more minutes. Serve garnished with strips of carrot and ginger root.

KITADA STORE

It's not hard to ignore Kitada Store going either way on Baldwin Avenue. You have to do a big U-turn and hunt down a parking place along the often crowded street. Makawao is the kind of Hawaiian ranch town whose western store fronts have attained a rustic charm and integrity over the years. The light green front of Kitada's almost blends with the hibiscus hedges that run along both sides. On the front window in faded gold script reads "Kau Kau," in Hawaii the equivalent of "good eats." Inside, the regulars, many of them construction workers grabbing an early breakfast of rice, eggs and Portuguese sausage or telephone repairmen on their coffee break, talk quietly in booths along one side of the room or from the benches provided before the formica-topped table in the center. Kitada is casual if nothing else. It closes stubbornly at 2 p.m. after lunch has been served. The old Japanese woman who takes your order has no one to please but herself. She's been doing this for too long, her miniscule body wrapped in a spotlessly starched white apron. Hung high up on the walls surrounding the room are a number of charcoal and pencil sketches of the store and other Makawao landmarks like the old theater across the street. All of them left by artists, good and indifferent, intrigued and wanting to give something back to the little store. To call Kitada's a store anymore is a misnomer. It's really a restaurant. A small steaming bowl of saimin made from real dried opai (shrimp) and floating with generous pieces of pork will only cost you a dollar. Paying for the bowl at the counter amid the trophies, candy boxes and turquoise T-shirts displaying an image of the store, you ask the woman how long the place has been here. She says it was once a grocery and then shrugs. They've had it since 1947. "Too long," she says.

34

WAIKAPU ZUCCHINI

1 cup chili sauce
2 teaspoons grated Parmesan
  cheese
2 tablespoons red wine vinegar
2 tablespoons olive oil

Salt and pepper to taste
Pinch of oregano
Pinch of garlic
Juice of ½ lemon
4 large zucchini

Using a whisk, mix all ingredients except the zucchini to make sauce. Wash and slice zucchini about ⅛" thick. Add to the sauce and chill for at least 4 hours, or longer, turning several times. This can be used as a salad, served on lettuce leaves, or as a relish on a buffet table. Serves 6-8.

WATER CHESTNUT SALAD

2 10-ounce packages frozen
   french cut green beans
1 5-ounce can water chestnuts
1 tablespoon sesame oil

2 tablespoons rice vinegar
2 tablespoons oyster sauce
2 tablespoons chopped green onions
White sesame seeds, toasted

Let beans defrost in a colander and pat dry. Slice water chestnuts into slivers. Mix together remaining ingredients except the sesame seeds and pour over the beans. Just before serving sprinkle sesame seeds over the top. Serves 6.

GREEK SALAD

4 large bell peppers, roasted
  (use red and green)
½ cup olive oil
3 tablespoons lemon juice
½ teaspoon dill weed
¼ teaspoon oregano
2 cloves garlic, finely chopped

¼ teaspoon salt
Freshly ground pepper
½ pound feta cheese
½ pound salami
1 large onion
Greek olives

Roast peppers by placing on a cookie sheet and broiling close to the flame, turning frequently until all the skin has blistered and blackened. Remove from the oven and put in a plastic bag until peppers are cool enough to handle. Remove skin, seeds and membranes and cut into one inch squares. Combine olive oil, lemon juice, dill weed, oregano, garlic, salt and pepper. Add peppers and marinate overnight. Several hours before serving drain the feta cheese and cut into equal size cubes. Cut salami and onion into equal size cubes. Drain Greek olives. Add the cheese, salami, onion and olives to the peppers. Refrigerate again until serving time. Serve on a bed of lettuce.

TARRAGON CHICKEN SALAD

¾ cup wild rice
2¼ cup water
Salt
2 cups diced poached chicken *
1 cup watercress leaves
½ cup thinly sliced green onion
½ cup diced celery
½ cup toasted blanched almonds,
    chopped

Dressing:
½ cup olive oil
¼ cup white wine vinegar
1 tablespoon chopped fresh tarragon
    or 1 teaspoon dried
1 teaspoon coarse salt
½ teaspoon freshly ground pepper

Rinse rice under running water. Bring 2¼ cups salted water to a rapid boil in medium saucepan over high heat. Stir in rice and return water to rapid boil. Stir rice with fork and reduce heat so water simmers gently. Cover and cook until grains puff open and white interior of rice appears, about 25-35 minutes. Rinse rice under cold water and drain well. Transfer to large bowl. Add chicken, watercress leaves, green onion, diced celery and chopped almonds. Combine ingredients for dressing. Mix well and add to salad. Toss gently and serve on a bed of lettuce. Serves 6.

*This is an extremely adaptable salad. It is good without any meat at all if you just want a vegetable salad. If you prefer some other meat to chicken, it is just as delicious with beef, ham, lamb or duck. Add more meat for a more substantial main course salad.

CAESAR SALAD

2 heads romaine, sliced in
  1 inch strips
½ cup chopped green onion
1 pound sliced bacon, cooked crisp,
  drained and chopped
1 cup croutons

Dressing:
½ cup olive oil
Juice of 2 lemons
½ teaspoon freshly ground pepper
¼ teaspoon chopped fresh mint
¾ teaspoon chopped fresh oregano
  or ¼ teaspoon dry
1 clove garlic, pressed
1 egg boiled for 1 minute
¾ teaspoon salt

Mix ingredients for the dressing in a bowl and whip vigorously. Mix lettuce and onions in a large salad bowl. When ready to serve, pour dressing over greens and toss. Sprinkle bacon over the top. Add croutons last. Toss again and serve immediately.

WAILEA PEA SALAD

1 10-ounce package frozen peas
1 cup celery
¼ cup green onions,
    including 3"-4" of green tops
1 cup macadamia nuts or cashews
¼ cup crisp bacon
1 cup sour cream
½ teaspoon salt
¼ cup Wailea Dressing

Wailea Dressing:
⅔ tablespoon lemon juice
1 cup red wine vinegar
1¼ tablespoon salt
1 teaspoon pepper
1 tablespoon Worchestershire sauce
1 teaspoon Dijon mustard
1 clove garlic
1 teaspoon sugar
3 cups corn oil

Combine ingredients for Wailea Dressing and set aside. Thaw the peas.
Chop celery, green onions, nuts and cooked bacon. Combine sour cream,
salt and ¼ cup Wailea Dressing. Mix lightly with the peas, celery, onions,
nuts and bacon. Chill. Serve on lettuce leaves. Serves 6.

WILD RICE SALAD

1 package wild rice and
  white rice mix
2 6-ounce jars marinated
  artichoke hearts
1 3-ounce jar pimento stuffed
  green olives

1 small green onion, chopped
¼ cup mayonnaise
¼ teaspoon salt
⅛ teaspoon pepper

Cook rice according to directions on the package. Drain and slice artichokes and olives. Mix with remaining ingredients. Check for seasoning. You may add some of the marinade from the artichokes for more dressing.

HANA FRUIT SALAD

2 large ripe papayas, peeled
   and sliced
2 ripe avocados, peeled and sliced
6 ripe tomatoes, peeled and sliced
1 small purple onion, sliced
   into thin rings
Bed of Boston or Manoa lettuce
2 teaspoons salt
1 teaspoon white pepper
½ teaspoon cracked black pepper

¼ teaspoon sugar
½ teaspoon dry mustard
Juice of ½ lemon
1 clove garlic, pressed
5 tablespoons tarragon vinegar
½ cup vegetable oil
2 tablespoons olive oil
1 coddled egg (boil for one minute)
   lightly beaten
½ cup light cream

Prepare the fruit and vegetables and arrange in sections on a platter. Combine remaining ingredients in a jar with a tightly fitting lid. Shake vigorously. Pour over sliced fruit and vegetables when ready to serve. Serves 6-8. The flavors of this particular combination are wonderful together and the ingredients, artistically arranged on a pretty platter make a beautiful salad.

POPPY SEED DRESSING

1¼ cup sugar
⅔ cup Japanese rice vinegar
1-2 tablespoons grated onion
1 tablespoon poppy seeds

2 teaspoons dry mustard
2 teaspoons salt
1 cup salad oil

Bring vinegar and sugar to a boil in a small saucepan. Cool. Pour mixture into a blender and blend in onion, dry mustard and salt. With blender running, slowly pour in oil. Just before turning off the blender, add the poppy seeds. Makes 2 cups. The Country Club serves this dressing with slices of papaya, banana, pineapple and orange topped with cottage cheese.

SPINACH SALAD

1 pound fresh spinach
6 mushrooms, sliced
1 cup water chestnuts, sliced
6 slices bacon, cooked crisp,
  then crumbled
¾ cup fresh bean sprouts
½ cup shredded Swiss cheese
½ cup thinly sliced Kula onion

Chutney Dressing:
¼ cup wine vinegar
¼ cup mango chutney, chopped
1 clove garlic, crushed
2 tablespoons coarsely ground
  French mustard
2 teaspoons sugar
⅓ – ½ cup vegetable oil
Salt and pepper

The salad ingredients can be prepared up to a day ahead, packaged separately in plastic bags and kept in the refrigerator. Toss all together with dressing when ready to serve. To make the Chutney Dressing combine vinegar, chutney, garlic, mustard and sugar in processor or blender. Mix briefly, add oil slowly until dressing is thick. Let stand 30 minutes at room temperature before serving. Dressing will keep a week in the refrigerator. Serves 8.

SOMEN NOODLE SALAD

1 9-ounce package somen noodles
1 package bean sprouts
¾ pound fresh ground pork
Chopped green onion

Dressing:
2 tablespoons garlic oil*
¾ cup oyster sauce
½ teaspoon sugar
1-2 tablespoons shoyu
1 tablespoon sesame oil

Mix salad dressing ingredients together and set aside. In a large kettle bring water to boil. Set a colander in the water, add the ground pork and cook until pork turns white. Keep the water boiling and lift the colander out, draining pork as you lift it out. Put pork in a bowl, return colander to the boiling water, add bean sprouts and cook for 1 minute. Remove colander, draining bean sprouts and plunge them into cold water. Drain again. Using the same boiling water, cook the somen noodles for about 3 minutes, or until done. Drain the noodles and run under cold water. Drain again. To avoid crushing the delicate noodles use your fingers to mix noodles, pork and bean sprouts together with the dressing. Garnish with the chopped green onions. Serve cold or at room temperature. This can be made ahead and refrigerated, but it does not keep over 24 hours. Serves 4-6.

*Put a clove of garlic peeled and crushed in ¼ cup oil and let it sit overnight.

24 HOUR COLE SLAW

1 medium cabbage, shredded
½ cup sugar
2 medium white onions,
  sliced into rings
1 teaspoon celery seed

1 teaspoon sugar
1½ teaspoon salt
1 teaspoon dry mustard
1 cup white vinegar
1 cup salad oil

Stir ½ cup sugar into the shredded cabbage and place half the mixture into a large bowl. Cover with onion rings and then with the remaining cabbage. Combine celery seed, sugar, salt, mustard and vinegar in a saucepan and bring to full boil. Stir in 1 cup of salad oil and bring to a boil again. Pour the dressing over the cabbage. DO NOT STIR. Cover and refrigerate for twenty-four hours. This cole slaw keeps for several weeks in the refrigerator. Serves 6.

TOFU SALMON SALAD

1 16-ounce block of tofu
¾ cup shoyu
1 tablespoon sesame oil
1 tablespoon lemon juice
½ cup salad oil

2 cups shredded lettuce
2 medium tomatoes
2 stalks green onion
1 6½-ounce can pink salmon

Put tofu in a colander over a bowl in the refrigerator and allow to drain 2-3 hours. While the tofu is draining, mix together shoyu, sesame oil and lemon juice. Heat the salad oil in a saucepan until it first bubbles and then smokes. Place the pot in the sink over a wooden board and carefully pour shoyu sauce mixture into the pot. Return the saucepan to the burner and cook for a few seconds. Cool and then chill. When tofu is well drained, remove from refrigerator and cut into ½" cubes. Using a large shallow casserole, layer: lettuce, tofu, salmon, tomatoes and green onion. Just before serving, pour desired amount of sauce over salad. Serves 6.

MANDARIN CHICKEN SALAD

1 11-ounce can mandarin
  oranges
½ cup syrup from oranges
1½ envelopes unflavored gelatin
¾ cup white wine
1 teaspoon powdered chicken
   broth base
½ teaspoon salt

½ teaspoon curry powder
¼ cup chopped chutney
1 tablespoon chopped scallions
1 cup sour cream
1 cup chopped cooked chicken
½ cup chopped water chestnuts
2 tablespoons wine vinegar
Lettuce or watercress

Drain the oranges, saving ½ cup of the orange syrup. Place syrup, wine and gelatin in a saucepan. Stir over low heat until gelatin is dissolved. Remove from heat. Add chicken broth base, salt, curry powder, chutney and scallions. Chill until partially set (about 15 minutes). Blend in sour cream and fold in orange segments, chicken, water chestnuts and vinegar. Place in 6-cup oiled ring mold and refrigerate until set. Unmold on bed of lettuce or watercress. Serves 6.

OAT GROAT SALAD

4 cups boiling water
2 cups oat groats
1 teaspoon salt
3 tablespoons wine vinegar
2 tablespoons lemon juice
1 teaspoon Worchestershire sauce
½ cup salad oil
2 cucumbers, peeled, seeded
    and sliced thin

⅔ cup thinly sliced radishes
⅔ cup minced green pepper
⅔ cup thinly sliced celery
3 tablespoons minced fresh
    parsley
3 tablespoons minced fresh
    tarragon
1 tablespoon minced fresh chives

Bring water to boil in a saucepan. Stir in groats and salt, partially cover and cook one hour. Drain in colander and rinse under cold water. Set colander over saucepan of water and steam, covered with dish towel and lid, 10-15 minutes or until fluffy and dry. In a large bowl whisk together vinegar, lemon juice and Worcestershire sauce. Add oil in a slow stream, beating until emulsified. Season with salt and pepper to taste. Add groats while warm and stir to mix. Add cucumbers, radishes, green peppers, celery and herbs. Combine well and let sit at room temperature for one hour. Serves 8.

CHINESE CHICKEN SALAD

½ pound cooked boned chicken
  breasts, shredded
1 small head iceberg lettuce,
  shredded
4 stalks green onions cut into
  2" strips, then sliced thin
2 tablespoons toasted almonds,
  chopped or slivered
2 tablespoons toasted white
  sesame seeds, slightly crushed
1 2½-ounce can chow mein noodles
Chinese parsley, optional

Dressing:
2 teaspoons salt
1 teaspoon pepper
6 tablespoons vinegar
4 tablespoons sugar
½ teaspoon MSG (optional)
½ cup salad oil

Combine chicken, lettuce, green onions, almonds, sesame seeds. Mix well.
Chow mein noodles should be added in the last minute. Make dressing by
combining salt, pepper, vinegar, sugar, MSG, and salad oil. Mix well and
pour over salad just before serving. Toss and garnish with Chinese parsley if
desired.

CHICKEN NAMASU

3 whole chicken breasts
4 cucumbers
½ cup sugar
½ cup shoyu
½ cup white vinegar
½ cup sesame oil*
3 tablespoons toasted sesame seeds

4 stalks green onion, finely chopped
4 cloves garlic, minced
1 or 2 Hawaiian red chili peppers,
 seeded and minced
1 tablespoon hondashi
 (powdered Japanese stock base)

Simmer chicken breasts in salted water until tender, 15-20 minutes. Set aside until cool enough to handle. Remove the skin and bones from the chicken and pull the meat apart into long strips. Seed the cucumbers and cut into long strips 2″ long and ⅛″ thick. Combine the remaining ingredients to make the sauce. Just before serving toss the chicken and the cucumber strips with the sauce.

*This may seem like too much sesame oil, but the amount is correct and it is 100% pure sesame oil.

JUDY'S SPINACH SALAD

Salad Dressing:
⅓ cup salad oil
2 tablespoons wine vinegar
1 tablespoon white wine
1 teaspoon shoyu
½ teaspoon sugar
½ teaspoon dry mustard
¼ to ½ teaspoon curry powder

¼ teaspoon salt
¼ teaspoon garlic salt
½ teaspoon freshly ground pepper

1 pound fresh spinach
½ pound bacon
1 hard cooked egg, chopped

Make dressing and set aside. Cook bacon until crisp and crumble. Prepare spinach and tear into bite size pieces. Just before serving, toss with dressing and bacon. Top with chopped egg as a garnish. The addition of shoyu and curry powder to this dressing gives Judy's salad a unique island flavor. Serves 4-6.

KAUPO STORE

There's a wildness about Kaupo that's hard to describe. Tucked around the other side of Haleakala, the district that was once home to an entire community of Hawaiians has a feeling of vastness, a quiet sense of openness not common to islands. The old wood frame building that houses the Kaupo Store stands quietly along the County road which leads either to lush Kipahulu on one side or back to the arid beaches of Makena on the other. Between the store and the sea are over 200 acres of rolling pastureland with an old rock wall and a paddock belonging to the Kaupo Ranch. Kaupo can be windy and wild, but on this day the sky seems higher and the sun brighter than it does on any other spot on Maui. "There's not much of a business here anymore," says one ranch employee. The store, once owned and operated by the Soon family, is only open a few hours in the afternoon to cater to tourists who decided after reaching the seven sacred pools that they had just as well "go all the way around" to get back to their hotels. A retired policeman says he remembers "old man Soon" because he once ordered a model T Ford which arrived in parts and he assembled it himself outside the store. "He had a generator too," says the policeman, "and he hooked it up so that he could start it from inside the store and wouldn't have to go out and crank it up." Today, you can pick up some soda water, beer or canned goods you forgot in town; but not much more. But the benefits for those living in Kaupo have nothing to do with consumer goods.

KULA ONION CASSEROLE

¼ cup unsalted butter
7-8 large Kula onions, cut into
   large chunks
½ cup uncooked short grain rice

8 cups boiling salted water
1 cup grated Swiss cheese
⅔ cup half-and-half (light cream)
Salt and pepper to taste

Preheat oven to 325 degrees. Melt butter in a large skillet over medium heat. Add onions and saute until transparent. Cook rice in the boiling water for 5 minutes, then drain. Add rice, cheese and half and half to the onions. Pour into a shallow 2 quart dish and bake uncovered for 1 hour. This casserole is also excellent served cold with vinaigrette dressing: 6 tablespoons oil, 2 tablespoons white wine vinegar, 2 tablespoons fine herbes, salt and freshly ground pepper to taste. Serves 6-8.

KULA MARINATED VEGETABLES

½ cup vegetable oil
⅓ cup red wine vinegar
¼ cup minced fresh parsley
2 cloves garlic, minced
1 tablespoon Dijon mustard

1 heaping teaspoon honey
1½ teaspoons fresh chopped oregano
1½ teaspoons fresh chopped basil
1½ teaspoons fresh chopped tarragon
Salt and freshly ground pepper

Slice raw carrots, radishes, cauliflower, zucchini. Place in a bowl. Add whole stuffed green olives and pitted black olives, whole cherry tomatoes and blanched broccoli florets. You should have at least 8 cups of vegetables. Combine all ingredients for the marinade and blend well. Pour over the vegetables and chill at least 2 hours.

CARAWAY CABBAGE

2 tablespoons butter
4 teaspoons caraway seeds
1 small onion, diced
2 cloves garlic, minced

3 tablespoons cider vinegar
1 large head cabbage
1 cup sour cream
Salt and white pepper

Saute onion and garlic in butter until tender. Add vinegar and caraway seeds. Slice cabbage coarsely and add to onion and garlic mixture. Sprinkle with salt and simmer for 10 minutes. Add sour cream and simmer 10 minutes more. Add salt and white pepper to taste. This is a delicious hot vegetable. It is also good cold on a Rueben or ham sandwich.

ZUCCHINI AND PEA PUREE

1 cup chicken broth
1 10-ounce package frozen peas
3 shallots, peeled and sliced
2 small zucchini, thinly sliced

3 tablespoons butter
1 8-ounce can artichoke bottoms
Pine nuts for garnish (optional)
Salt to taste

In a saucepan bring the chicken broth to a simmer. Add the peas, shallots and zucchini and cook until tender, about 5 minutes. Drain. Put in a food processor and puree. Add 2 tablespoons butter and salt to taste. Set aside. Drain artichoke bottoms and saute in remaining butter until hot. Fill each one with puree and garnish with a few pine nuts, if desired. Use to garnish a platter of meat, or put in a casserole and serve as a separate vegetable.

BROCCOLI SOUFFLE

2 10-ounce packages frozen
   chopped broccoli
1 tablespoon wine vinegar
1 teaspoon Dijon mustard
6 egg whites
6 egg yolks

2 tablespoons flour
¼ teaspoon salt
½ teaspoon coarsely ground pepper
½ pound shredded Jack cheese
½ cup grated Parmesan cheese

Defrost broccoli and squeeze dry. Mix wine vinegar and mustard with broccoli and set aside. Beat egg whites until they hold soft peaks. Beat egg yolks with flour and salt until thick and lemon colored. Fold yolk mixture into whites. Spoon one third of the egg mixture into a greased 2 quart souffle dish. Arrange half the broccoli over the egg mixture and sprinkle with half the pepper, half the Jack cheese and a third of the Parmesan cheese. Cover with another third of the egg mixture and add the remaining broccoli, pepper and Jack cheese. Sprinkle with another third of the Parmesan cheese. Cover with the remaining egg mixture and sprinkle with the rest of the Parmesan cheese. Bake in a 350 degree oven for 25 minutes or until set in the center. Serve immediately. Serves 6-8.

CHINESE PEAS

2 tablespoons peanut oil
2 large Maui onions, chopped
¼ cup whole wheat flour
¼ cup tamari, or shoyu
¾ cup tomato juice

¾ cup water
2 pounds Chinese peas or snow peas
4 celery ribs, sliced in 1" pieces
2 large, firm tomatoes
½ cup white cheddar cheese, grated

Heat 1 tablespoon oil in large skillet over medium-high heat. Add onions and saute until tender. Reduce heat and add remaining oil. Slowly add flour, stirring constantly until flour is thoroughly mixed with onions. Slowly add tamari, tomato juice and water. Simmer 30 minutes, stirring often. Place peas and celery in a steamer or wok with rack and steam until just tender. Add tomatoes and steam 3 minutes more. Transfer to heated platter and pour sauce over the vegetables. Top with grated cheese. Serves 6-8. If you want to use this as an entree, you may use an assortment of vegetables and add more cheese on top.

CARROTS WITH VODKA

6 carrots
¼ cup vodka
½ teaspoon grated orange peel

1 tablespoon butter
Salt and pepper to taste
Parsley sprigs

Peel and julienne carrots. Put in a small baking dish with a tight cover. Add vodka and cook covered in a 350 degree oven for 1 hour. Season with butter, orange peel, salt and pepper. Garnish with parsley sprigs.

SWISS CHARD CASSEROLE

2 10-ounce packages frozen
   artichoke hearts
1½ pounds fresh swiss chard or
   spinach OR 2 packages frozen
   leaf spinach, thawed, squeezed
   dry and chopped
½ pound fresh mushrooms
4 tablespoons butter

1 tablespoon flour
½ cup milk
Garlic salt, salt and pepper to taste
1 14½-ounce can sliced tomatoes,
   drained
1 cup mayonnaise
1 cup sour cream
¼ cup lemon juice

Cook artichokes according to the directions on the package, drain and squeeze dry. Arrange artichoke hearts in flat bottom casserole (about 2 quart size). Blanch swiss chard, drain, squeeze dry and chop. Slice mushrooms and saute in butter. Make a white sauce with the flour, butter and milk. Season with salt, garlic salt and pepper. Mix swiss chard, ½ the mushrooms, tomatoes and white sauce together gently and pour over artichoke hearts in the casserole. Barely heat mayonnaise and sour cream, stirring gently. When warm, add lemon juice. Pour over vegetables. Garnish top with the remaining mushrooms. Bake at 350 degrees for 20-30 minutes. Serves 8-10 people. We were delighted with this unusual combination of flavors! Do try it with swiss chard. There are so few recipes for this delicious vegetable.

CARROTS PISTACHIO

6 carrots
½ cup water
½ teaspoon sugar
¼ cup pistachios, shelled

2 tablespoons butter
¼ cup Cointreau
Pinch of nutmeg

Peel and julienne carrots. Cook in ½ cup water to which you have added ½ teaspoon of sugar. When crisp-tender remove carrots from liquid and reduce liquid to 2 tablespoons. In a separate skillet saute pistachio nuts in 2 tablespoons of butter. Add the Cointreau. Mix nuts with carrots, add the 2 tablespoons carrot liquid, and a pinch of nutmeg. Quickly heat mixture again and serve.

TOFU WITH PEANUT SAUCE

1 pound tofu
1 4-ounce can straw mushrooms
2 tablespoons chopped green onion
Peanut Sauce:
2 tablespoons shoyu
3 tablespoons vegetable oil

½ cup finely chopped onion
½ cup water
¼ cup creamy peanut butter
2 tablespoons rice vinegar
½ teaspoon dried red pepper flakes
Salt

Heat shoyu and oil in small saucepan over medium heat. Add the onion and cook until limp. Reduce heat to low and add the water, peanut butter, vinegar, red pepper flakes, and salt to taste. Stir until smooth and set aside. Slice tofu in ½'' slices, pat dry and dredge in whole wheat flour. Heat small amount of vegetable oil in skillet. Fry tofu until just heated through and brown. Arrange slices on platter, put mushrooms on top and pour hot sauce over all. Sprinkle with chopped green onion.

HOT CHERRY TOMATOES

2 cups cherry tomatoes
1 cup whipping cream
2 tablespoons chopped mint

Drop tomatoes into boiling water, 3 or 4 at a time, for a few seconds—just long enough to loosen the skin. Remove from water and peel. In a small pan boil cream gently until it is reduced by half. Add the tomatoes and toss in the cream to coat and heat them through. Stir in the mint and serve immediately. This goes well with any roasted or broiled meat as the mint flavor is not very pronounced. To serve with lamb you might want to add 1 tablespoon more chopped mint.

VEGETABLE DRESSING

1¼ cups mayonnaise
½ cup vegetable oil
¼ cup honey
¼ cup prepared mustard
¼ teaspoon curry

3 tablespoons fresh lemon juice
2 green onions, finely chopped
1 tablespoon parsley, chopped
1 teaspoon celery seed
¼ teaspoon dry mustard

Combine all ingredients and chill. Makes 2 cups. Serve on broccoli, asparagus, or salad. This is a versatile vegetable dressing. It can be used with hot or cold vegetables – even on a hot baked potato.

LEMON BROCCOLI CROWN

3½ pounds broccoli with 4 inch stalk
2-3 tablespoons butter for bowl
8-10 very thin slices of lemon for garnish

Peel broccoli. Cut into 2″ florets. Cut stalks into 2″ lengths and quarter lengthwise. Blanch broccoli. Drain well and return to heat to evaporate any remaining liquid. Butter a 3 quart stainless steel mixing bowl 11″ in diameter. Line bowl with florets, flower side down. Fill in spaces between the floret stems with the stalk pieces. Cover with foil. (This can be done the day before and refrigerated. Bring to room temperature before continuing.) Set bowl of broccoli in a deep baking pan with enough boiling water to come about 2″ up the sides of the mixing bowl. Bake for 15 minutes at 350 degrees. Holding hand over foil, drain broccoli. Discard foil. Invert broccoli onto a serving platter, refitting any pieces that may have fallen out of place. Spoon Lemon Sauce over the top and garnish with lemon slices.

LEMON SAUCE

½ cup unsalted butter
⅓ cup dry vermouth
2 tablespoons fresh lemon juice
⅛ teaspoon freshly grated nutmeg
Salt and white pepper

Cut butter into ½" pieces and chill. Combine vermouth and lemon juice in saucepan and cook over a medium-high heat until reduced to 2 tablespoons, about 5 minutes. Remove from heat. Add 2 tablespoons of butter. Whisk quickly until just blended. Place over low heat and whisk in remaining butter, 1 piece at a time. Butter should thicken the sauce without melting into it. If at any time the sauce begins to separate, remove from the heat and whisk in 2 pieces of butter. Add nutmeg and season to taste with white pepper. This can be made up to 2 hours ahead and kept warm in a water bath. This is really worth the effort. It is an elegant vegetable presentation.

MAALAEA STORE

The Maalaea Store also known as Jimmy's, nestled in the elbow of an area of land between the Lahaina pali and the Kihei mudflats, once commanded a view of the fishing and leisure boats it served. Today that view is obscured by a row of concrete buildings and the private dwellings along the beach running toward Kihei have been replaced by high rise condominiums. Family owned for most of this century, the Maalaea Store is still in its original wooden structure. The gas pump out front is a reminder of the days when the store was the final stop before the winding, dusty trip along the old pali road to Lahaina. The goods inside have changed with the times. Where once housewives from the plantation camp near Waikapu shopped for bolts of brightly colored cotton, there are now yards of fishing line, boat epoxy and shiny flecked flies pretending to be tiny squid. The local residents still stop by for the cold drinks now held in modern upright refrigerators and to fill up on steaming hot dogs near the entrance. The hot dogs hold the same allure here for many that they do at a major league baseball game on the Mainland. While they appear to be nothing special – just a little mustard, catsup and pickle relish – to their devotees they have reached culinary heights. The little store closes down tight on Monday giving everyone a rest. But in the noontime Sunday sun two young, brown, waterlogged surfers sit in front on the makeshift benches trying to keep the popsicles they're eating from running down their arms and stare wordlessly out to sea saying a quiet little prayer for waves.

GLOSSARY OF ISLAND FISH

AU (Kajiki) – Swordfish or Marlin

AHI (Shibi) – Tuna. There are three kinds—yellow fin, blue fin, albacore. Best for sashimi.

AKULE (Aji) – Big-eyed Scad.

AHOLEHOLE – Mountain bass

AMAAMA (Bora or Ina) – Mullet. Two kinds—fresh and salt water.

AWA – Milk fish. Use to make fishcake.

EHU – Red snapper.

KAHALA – Amber Fish or Yellow Tail

KAKU (Kamasu) – Barracuda

KUMU – Goatfish. Dark salmon – colored with light brownish-red back.

HAPUUPUU (Ara) – Sea bass

HEE (Tako) – Octopus

HUA IA (Kazunoko) – Fish Roe

MAHIMAHI (Mansaku) – Dolphin.

MANINI – Angel fish, Coral fish or Butterfly fish

MIKIAWA (Iwashi) – Hawaiian Sardine

MOANA – Goatfish. This one is salmon-colored with black spots.

MOI – Threadfish.

MUHEE (Ika) – Cuttlefish

NEHU (Iriko) – Type of anchovy

OIO – Bone fish. Used to make fishcake

OPELU (Maru Aji) – Mackerel Scad. From mackerel family.

ONO (Sawara) – Wahoo. Belongs to the Barracuda family.

OPAKAPAKA – Pink Snapper.

PAPIO – Cravally. Baby ulua.

UHU – Parrot Fish. Green type and red type. Red is not as common.

UKU – Snapper. Grayish fish.

ULAULA KOAE (Onaga) – Snapper.

UU (Menpachi) – Squirrel Fish.

ULUA (Hoshi ulua) – Pompano. Baby ulua called papio.

WEKE – Goatfish. Salmon-colored with yellow streak.

BAKED AHI

4 ahi fillets, ½" thick
1½ teaspoons minced shallots
¼ pound fresh mushrooms, sliced
½ cup dry white wine

¼ cup whipping cream
1 tablespoon butter
Salt and pepper to taste
Minced parsley

Butter a shallow skillet large enough to arrange the fillets side by side without overlapping. Sprinkle with salt and pepper. Arrange fillets over bottom of skillet and top with sliced mushrooms and shallots. Pour wine over all. Cut waxed paper to fit the skillet; butter one side of the paper and put it snuggly over the fish, buttered side against the fish. Heat skillet over medium high heat. The minute the liquid starts to bubble, check the time and cook for 3½ minutes. Test for doneness by pressing on the fish. It should feel firm and bouncy, with an opaque look. If it looks pink, it is not done—return to heat and cook another minute or so. When it is done, remove to a platter and keep warm. Add cream to the juices in the skillet and bring to a low boil. Pour over fish on platter (the sauce will be thin) and garnish with parsley. Serve immediately.

MAALAEA GINGER FISH

4 tablespoons butter
2 large cloves garlic, minced
1 3-4 pound whole fish,
   (Opakapaka, Onaga, Moilua, etc.)

¼ cup chopped ginger root
½ cup white wine
¼ cup lemon juice
1 4-ounce can straw mushrooms
Brown Sauce*

Make garlic butter with first two ingredients and rub outside of fish generously, saving a little to butter inside of wrapping foil. Place fish on greased foil and sprinkle inside cavity and outside with chopped ginger, white wine and lemon juice. Wrap securely and bake in 400 degree oven approximately 30 minutes. Serve whole with sauce, garnished with straw mushrooms. For the sauce combine ¾ cup baking liquid, 2 tablespoons oyster sauce and ⅓ cup brown sauce.

*For the brown sauce chop 3-4 fresh mushrooms and cook in ⅓ cup dry sherry until sherry is reduced by one-half. Strain and set liquid aside. In a saucepan melt 1½ tablespoons butter. Add 1½ tablespoons flour and cook over low heat, stirring constantly until color becomes light tan. Add 2 cups strong beef broth. Bring to a boil and cook 3-5 minutes, stirring constantly, then simmer for 30 minutes. Add sherry, simmer a bit more and use in your fish sauce. (If you are in a hurry, you can use a package of brown sauce mix.) This delicious fish is one of the specialties at the Waterfront Restaurant in Maalaea.

SCALLOPS SAUTE

1½ pounds scallops
1 pound fresh mushrooms, sliced
3 cloves garlic

⅓ cup finely chopped parsley
7 tablespoons unsalted butter
Flour

Quickly saute mushrooms in 1 tablespoon of butter. Set aside. Mince together garlic and parsley. Pat the scallops with a paper towel to make sure they are dry and dust lightly with flour. Saute in remaining 6 tablespoons of butter for several minutes. Add parsley and garlic mixture and the mushrooms. Cook, stirring carefully, JUST until the scallops are opaque, about 2-3 minutes. Watch carefully—scallops become tough when they are overcooked. Season with salt and pepper and serve. Serves 6.

FISH CHINESE STYLE

1 8-ounce fillet of white fish (ono)
1 teaspoon sugar
2 tablespoons shoyu
1 teaspoon grated garlic

1 tablespoon grated ginger
⅓ cup chopped green onion
3 tablespoons oil
Sprigs of cilantro for garnish

Saute fillet in butter until just done, about 5 minutes—do not overcook. Put on serving plate. Sprinkle the following ingredients separately on top of fish: sugar, shoyu, garlic, ginger and green onion. Heat oil until almost smoking. Slowly, a tablespoon at a time, drizzle over the fish and topping to sear them all. Put a sprig of cilantro on top and serve immediately. This is for one serving. It can, of course, be prepared for as many people as you wish, using the above formula for each serving.

SHRIMP SAGANAKI

1 pound raw medium shrimp
1 10-ounce package frozen
    artichoke hearts
Boiling salted water
4 tablespoons olive oil
¼ pound small whole mushrooms

2 cloves garlic, finely minced
½ teaspoon salt
Freshly ground pepper
½ teaspoon crumbled dried oregano
2 tablespoons lemon juice
2 tablespoons finely chopped parsley

Peel and devein shrimp. Blanch artichoke hearts in boiling salted water for 2 minutes, then drain. Heat olive oil in a frying pan, add shrimp and mushrooms and cook until shrimp turns pink. Add artichoke hearts, garlic, salt, pepper and oregano. Heat until everything is hot. Sprinkle with lemon juice and stir lightly to blend flavors. Sprinkle with parsley. This is good as an appetizer or light entree.

GREEN PEPPERCORN SCALLOPS

1 pound scallops
Salt and pepper to taste
Flour
¼ cup butter
1½ teaspoons chopped shallots
3 medium fresh mushrooms

2 teaspoons green Madagascar
  peppercorns, lightly crushed
2 tablespoons sauterne wine
1 tablespoon lemon juice
1 teaspoon chopped parsley

Season scallops with salt, pepper. Dust lightly with flour. Melt 3 table-spoons of the butter in skillet; add scallops. Brown them evenly on all sides until almost done, about 2 minutes. In separate skillet heat remaining 1 tablespoon butter, add shallots, mushrooms, peppercorns, wine and lemon juice. Simmer to reduce liquid. When mushrooms are tender add scallops; mix well. Sprinkle with chopped parsley and serve. May be garnished with 1 lemon, sprig of parsley, and cherry tomatoes, slightly sauteed. Serves 2.

SALMON IN PASTRY

2 tablespoons butter, melted
1 onion, finely chopped
1 10-ounce package frozen
   chopped spinach, thawed
1 3-ounce package cream cheese
Salt and pepper to taste

1 package of 6 frozen patty shells
1 16-ounce can red salmon
1 lemon
½ cup Parmesan cheese, grated
1 egg white, beaten

Saute onions in butter until translucent. Add spinach and cook over low heat for 5 minutes. Add cream cheese, salt and pepper and continue cooking until cheese is melted. Remove from heat and set aside. Unwrap patty shells and let thaw slightly. Roll on floured board into 6″ or 8″ squares. Place a portion of salmon in the middle of each square and squeeze lemon over it. Add equal portions of the spinach mixture. Place 1 tablespoon Parmesan cheese on each. Bring outer edges into center and squeeze together. Brush with beaten egg white. Bake at 450 degrees for 10-15 minutes. Serves 6. This may be served with a white sauce combined with mushrooms, Cheddar cheese and paprika.

POACHED FISH

1½ - 2 pounds thick fish fillet
  (opakapaka or mahi mahi)
4 - 6 fresh fennel bulbs, tops and
  outer leaves trimmed
1¼ cup chicken broth
½ cup onion, chopped

1 bay leaf
4 peppercorns
1 cup white wine
1 cup water
½ cup whipping cream

Wash fennel, cut to ¾ inch of bulb, discard tough stems and roots and cut bulbs in half lengthwise. In a 10″ - 12″ frying pan bring broth to a boil. Add fennel cut side down, cover and simmer gently until tender, about 10 minutes. Remove from pan and keep warm. Using the same pan, add the chopped onion, bay leaf, peppercorns, wine and water. Bring to a boil and add fish. Cover and simmer until fish is almost opaque in the thickest part. Lift fish from pan, arrange on platter, surround with fennel pieces, cover and keep warm while you make the sauce. On highest heat boil cooking liquid uncovered to reduce to ¾ cup (about 5 minutes). Add cream, stirring and boiling until sauce is again reduced to ¾ cup. Spoon sauce around fish and fennel. Garnish with a few fresh fennel leaves and serve. Serves 4.

CHINESE CHICKEN

1 frying chicken
¼ cup shoyu
1 piece ginger the size of a
   quarter, diced

2 green onions cut in 2 inch lengths,
   then sliced lengthwise
½ cup peanut oil, smoking hot

Bring a large pot of water to boil and put chicken in. As soon as it stops boiling, remove chicken. Bring water to a boil again. Put chicken in again. Turn heat off. Cover tightly and let sit for 1¼ hours. Remove chicken, skin and bone, leaving meat in fairly large pieces. Arrange pieces on a platter. Sprinkle with ginger, green onions and shoyu. Pour hot oil over all and serve immediately.

BAKED CHICKEN AND GARLIC

4-5 pounds chicken thighs
½ cup cooking oil
4 ribs of celery, cut lengthwise
2 medium onions, chopped
6 sprigs of parsley
1 teaspoon tarragon

½ cup dry vermouth
2½ teaspoons salt
¼ teaspoon freshly ground pepper
4 heads of garlic (about 40 cloves),
    separated but unpeeled

Put celery, onions, parsley and tarragon in the bottom of a 6 quart casserole. Coat the chicken pieces evenly and thoroughly with the oil and lay them on the vegetables in the casserole. Pour the vermouth over the chicken and sprinkle with salt, pepper and a dash of nutmeg. Place the garlic cloves around the chicken pieces. Cover casserole tightly using foil AND a lid. Bake at 375 degrees for 1½ hours without removing the lid. Serve the chicken directly from the casserole with thin slices of warm French bread or toast. Make sure each person has some garlic cloves to squeeze out of the husks onto the bread to eat with the chicken.

CHICKEN CARA MIA

6 chicken thighs
¼ cup vegetable oil
½ small onion, sliced
1 clove garlic, minced
1 10-ounce can tomatoes

1 6-ounce jar marinated artichoke
  hearts
1 teaspoon basil
½ cup chopped parsley
Salt and pepper

Place tomatoes in a bowl and squeeze until they are a soupy consistency. Set aside. Brown chicken thighs in oil. Remove from heat and set aside. Saute onion and garlic in the same oil. Add the tomatoes and their juice, the artichoke hearts with the marinade, ¼ cup parsley, the basil, and salt and pepper to taste. Place chicken thighs on top of the mixture. Cover and simmer for 45 minutes. Sprinkle top with reserved parsley and serve with hot rice or pasta. Serves 4.

SWISS CHICKEN CASSEROLE

4 whole chicken breasts, boned
  and skinned
1 10½-ounce can cream of
  chicken soup

2 cups fresh mushrooms, sliced
8 ounces Swiss cheese, sliced
2 cups herbed stuffing mix
½ cup butter

Cut chicken into large pieces and place in bottom of a 2 quart baking dish. Spread cream of chicken soup over chicken pieces. Add sliced mushrooms, sliced Swiss cheese and stuffing mix which has been crushed into crumbs. Dot with ½ cup butter, cover, and bake at 350 degrees for 35 minutes. Serves 6.

CHICKEN ENCHILADAS

1½ pounds boned chicken breasts
1 cup chicken stock
6 ounces cream cheese
2 cups heavy cream
¾ cup finely chopped onion
6 green peppers, roasted, skinned,
  seeded and chopped
2 medium fresh green tomatoes,
  skinned and chopped

1 4-ounce can diced green chilies
2 tablespoons coarsely chopped
  fresh cilantro
1 egg
1½ teaspoon salt
¼ teaspoon pepper
3 tablespoons oil
12 corn tortillas
⅓ cup Parmesan cheese, grated

Simmer chicken breasts in chicken stock until tender. Cool and shred. Reserve stock. In a large mixing bowl beat cream cheese until smooth. Gradually add ½ cup cream. Stir in onions and chicken. Mix thoroughly and set aside. To make sauce, put chilies, 6 green peppers, tomatoes, cilantro and ¼ cup reserved stock in the bowl of a food processor. Puree until smooth. Add the remaining 1½ cup cream, 1 egg, salt and pepper. Blend 10 seconds more. Scrape into a large bowl. In a heavy 8″ – 10″ frying pan heat oil over moderate heat, soften tortillas one at a time in the hot oil. Remove from pan allowing the oil to drain off tortilla. Dip tortilla in sauce and fill with ¼ cup chicken mixture, roll up and place seam side down in a shallow 8″ x 10″ baking dish. Pour any remaining sauce over the tortilla rolls, sprinkle with Parmesan cheese and bake on the middle shelf of the oven at 350 degrees for 15 minutes. Serves 6-8.

LYCHEE CHICKEN

1 to 3 pounds of boneless chicken
1 5-ounce can water chestnuts, chopped
1 small onion, chopped
2 tablespoons oil
1 15-ounce can lychees
2 tablespoons cornstarch
½ teaspoon salt

2 tablespoons shoyu
1 tablespoon sherry
2 egg whites
1 tablespoon oil
2 teaspoons cornstarch
1 tablespoon shoyu
¼ cup chicken stock
½ cup lychee juice reserved from can

Cut chicken into bite size pieces. Mix together cornstarch, salt, shoyu, sherry and egg whites. Pour over chicken and let stand at least ½ hour. Heat 2 tablespoons oil in frying pan and brown the chicken pieces. Add water chestnuts and onion and cook for 15 minutes. Place on serving platter. Drain lychees, reserving ½ cup juice, and arrange on top. Keep warm. Mix 1 tablespoon oil, 2 teaspoons cornstarch, 1 tablespoon shoyu, ¼ cup chicken stock and ½ cup lychee juice in frying pan and cook until sauce thickens. Pour over chicken and lychees and serve immediately. Serves 4-6.

GUAMANIAN CHICKEN

10 pounds chicken thighs
2½ cups shoyu
Juice of 20 fresh limes (about 1 cup)
1 cup catsup
1 cup sugar
1 onion, chopped
Rinds of 5 squeezed limes

Finadene Sauce:
3 tablespoons shoyu
¼ cup lime juice
¼ cup chopped onions
3 small red peppers, seeded and
    crushed with ¼ teaspoon salt OR
    Tabasco to taste

Mix together shoyu, lime juice, catsup, sugar, onion and lime rinds. Place chicken pieces in a large container, add marinade and keep in the refrigerator, covered, from one to three days. When ready to cook, drain off marinade, bring chicken to room temperature, and broil. It is best done over a low charcoal fire, but is fine done in the oven broiler too. To prepare sauce combine shoyu, lime juice, chopped onion, red peppers. Put cooked chicken on a platter and serve with the sauce on the side. This is perfect for a big summer barbecue. It is easy to prepare and the lime juice seems to cook the chicken a bit so it does not need as long a time on the grill – the flavor is addicting!

CHICKEN LUAU

3 10-ounce packages leaf spinach
3 pounds chicken breasts, boned
  and skinned
1 teaspoon salt
1 12-ounce can coconut milk

1 10½-ounce can cream of
  chicken soup
4 tablespoons flour
¼ cup Parmesan cheese

Thaw spinach, squeeze dry and chop coarsely. Put spinach in a well greased casserole. Arrange chicken pieces on top of the spinach. Mix the soup, the coconut milk, salt and the flour and pour over chicken and spinach. Sprinkle cheese over the top and bake uncovered at 350 degrees for 1¼ hours. Serves 6.

TURKEY KEBABS

3 tablespoons dry sherry
3 tablespoons dark brown sugar
½ cup peanut oil
⅔ cup shoyu
1 tablespoon minced ginger
1 clove garlic, minced
1 teaspoon grated lemon rind
1 teaspoon red pepper flakes

1 Maui onion, minced
3 pounds turkey breast, skinned, boned and cubed
1 large Maui onion, cut in chunks for skewer
2 large zucchini, cut crosswise
12 large cherry tomatoes
1 tablespoon minced fresh parsley

Combine sherry, sugar, oil, shoyu, ginger, garlic, lemon rind, red pepper flakes and minced onion. Put turkey cubes in a shallow glass dish in one layer and pour marinade over it. Marinate at room temperature at least 4 hours or chilled overnight. Blanch the zucchini, drain and rinse with cold water. Thread six metal skewers with turkey and vegetables, baste with marinade and broil for 4 minutes. Turn and baste the other side and broil for 4 minutes more. Transfer to a heated platter and sprinkle with parsley. Serves 6.

PORTLOCK DUCK

1 6-pound duck with giblets
½ cup brandy
½ cup parsley, minced
6 green onions, chopped
1 10½-ounce can consomme

1 bay leaf
Salt and pepper
½ pound fresh mushrooms, sliced
1 tablespoon cornstarch
¼ cup water

Thaw duck if necessary and reserve giblets. In a large, deep frying pan slowly fry whole duck, turning often and pricking the skin to let the fat run out. (This will take at least an hour.) When the skin is brown and crispy remove pan from fire, drain off the fat and pour the brandy over the duck. Cover and let sit for 15 minutes. Add parsley, green onions, consomme, bay leaf, salt and pepper. Simmer covered 1½ hours, adding water if necessary. A half an hour before serving add the mushrooms, chopped gizzard and heart. Fifteen minutes before serving add chopped liver, a dash of brandy and the cornstarch mixed with water. Stir and simmer until thickened. Serve in slices on large croutons made by frying slices of French bread slowly in butter until toasted, and accompanied with applesauce seasoned to taste with horseradish. A pickled peach is also a nice accompaniment if available. Serves 3-4.

BANANAS

Scalloped Bananas:
¼ cup evaporated milk
1½ teaspoon salt

¾ cup fine cornflake crumbs
6 firm, not too ripe bananas

Mix milk and salt. Cut peeled bananas into pieces 2-3 inches long. Dip into milk and roll in crumbs. Fry in butter until crust is nicely brown and crisp. Delicious with poultry, pork or curry.

Baked Bananas:
1 banana per person

Butter

Be sure to use very ripe bananas. Wash skin and put bananas, unpeeled, into pan with a little water in it. Bake at 350 degrees for 20 minutes. Serve like a baked potato, splitting the skin and putting a pat of butter to melt inside.

WILLOW'S CURRY SAUCE

3 tablespoons butter
3 garlic cloves, peeled and
  finely chopped
1 inch slice of fresh ginger,
  peeled and finely chopped
1 small onion, peeled and finely
  chopped

1 teaspoon salt
1 tablespoon sugar
1 tablespoon curry powder
4 tablespoons flour
1 quart frozen coconut milk
4 cups cooked chicken

Melt butter. Add garlic, ginger and onion. Saute for a few minutes. Add salt, sugar, curry powder and flour. Mix thoroughly. Add coconut milk a little at a time, stirring to a smooth thickness and cook for about 20 minutes. Let sauce stand for several hours. When ready to serve, strain, reheat and add the chicken. This superb sauce is also good with shrimp, lamb or turkey.

HONOLUA STORE

Caught squarely between two cultures, the Honolua Store stands big, brown and shingled alongside the lush, well-manicured greens and fairways of the posh Kapalua resort. Next door, looking too new, close and out-of-scale is a sweepingly modern concrete church. Slated for extinction in 1983 after 65 years of business, the store was rescued by Maui Land and Pineapple Company. Today, instead of the mercantile items and hundreds of plate lunches sold to plantation families, surfers and construction workers, there are bottles of European and California vintage wines and an amusingly disproportionate number of pimento filled olives and tiny cocktail onions. Basic foodstuff like eggs, milk and fresh fruit are still there, only today among them is a flaky sweet chocolate croissant. Outside on the ancient wooden benches facing the gas pumps two Hawaiian boys finish the last of their packages of rock salt plum under posters advertising the latest rock group to play the Lahaina Civic Amphitheater and aerobic classes held on weekday mornings for those with the leisure time to attend. Two young women with sun streaked hair wearing bright crisp golf clothes pull up in front in a cart and dash up the stairs for some sun block without paying much attention to the interior which, while less jammed with goods needed by plantation families, hasn't changed much. The office is still. Its old, dark, weathered desks and equipment look tired. An archaic, wheeled ladder hooks to a track rod running high along the ceiling enabling it to slide along the half empty shelves. The country store which once served the humble plantation villages of the West Side now serves the jet set too with its own brand of country chic.

GRILLED HAM STEAKS

1 center cut ham steak, 1" thick
½ cup dry red wine
½ cup guava jelly (or current jelly)
1 tablespoon Dijon mustard

Grill ham steak over a charcoal fire, low enough so the meat won't burn, for 30-40 minutes. While the ham is cooking, heat the wine, jelly and mustard in a pan large enough to hold the ham steak. When the meat is brown, add it to the sauce, cover and simmer for 30 minutes, either on a cool part of the grill or on the stove. Cut into slices and serve. Serves 4-6.

SWEETBREADS

2 pounds sweetbreads
Water
2 tablespoons vinegar
¼ pound butter
½ pound mushrooms, sliced
Salt and pepper

5 green onions, chopped
¼ to ½ cup vermouth
Thin sliced sourdough bread or
   french bread
Butter

Soak sweetbreads in cold water for 1 hour. Drain. Put in pot and barely cover with cold water. Add 2 tablespoons of vinegar. Very slowly bring up to a simmer but do not boil. Cook gently until just done, about 20 minutes. Plunge into cold water. Remove all membranes and veins and either slice or break into pieces. Melt butter in a pan and brown sweetbreads. Add mushrooms, adding more butter if needed. Add salt and pepper to taste and chopped green onions. Saute one minute. Add vermouth and cook one more minute. Serve immediately on croutons. Croutons: Thinly slice bread and lightly butter one side of the slice. Place on baking sheet and put in a 200 degree oven until crisp and starting to brown — two or more hours. Serves 6.

PORK HASH

1 pound ground pork
½ pound raw Chinese fish cake mix
1 chung choi*
1 cup water chestnuts, chopped

4 tablespoons shoyu
2 eggs
4 green onions, chopped
4 tablespoons oyster sauce

Mix all ingredients together in a bowl. If you are using for stuffing, stuff lightly into turkey cavity. This is an old island recipe—so different from the common bread stuffing. Be sure to save the carcass for soup (see our recipe for Jook). This versatile recipe is also excellent served as a pupu when stuffed in aburage halves, steamed for 45 minutes and served with the juices from the pan thickened with a little cornstarch mixed with water.

*Salted cabbage, found in packages in the oriental section of the market.

EGGPLANT KUO

4 long eggplants
⅓ pound ground pork
1 tablespoon chopped green
   onion
1 tablespoon finely chopped
   ginger

1 tablespoon finely chopped
   garlic
1 tablespoon sherry
2 tablespoons shoyu
2 teaspoons sugar
1 cup cooking oil

Cut each unpeeled eggplant lengthwise down the middle. Cut both halves into 3″ lengths. Heat oil in wok or large skillet. Saute eggplant for about 3 minutes, then drain on absorbant paper. Remove all but 2 tablespoons of oil from the pan and fry onion, ginger and garlic for 1 minute. Add pork and stir fry until thoroughly cooked. Add eggplant and shoyu, sugar and sherry. Lower heat and simmer 3 minutes. Serve with rice. Serves 4.

MUI SHIU PORK

½ pound chop suey style pork
1 tablespoon cooking oil
10 green onions, shredded
½ head cabbage, shredded
4 large dried mushrooms
2 tablespoons dried shrimp
1 5-ounce can water chestnuts,
  chopped
¼ to½ teaspoon chili paste
  with garlic*

1 teaspoon oyster sauce
1 teaspoon sesame oil
1 tablespoon shoyu
1 teaspoon sugar
1 tablespoon cornstarch
1 tablespoon sherry
8-12 teaspoons hoi sin sauce
8-12 flour tortillas

A half an hour before cooking, marinate pork in mixture of sugar, cornstarch, sherry and shoyu, and soak mushrooms and shrimp in enough water to cover them. Heat 1 tablespoon cooking oil in a wok or skillet and brown pork. Drain mushrooms and shrimp, reserving the liquid. Chop shrimp and slice mushrooms. Add ½ cup of the liquid to the pork. Cover and simmer for 10 minutes. Add shrimp and chili paste, stir, remove from wok and set aside. Put 1 tablespoon reserved liquid into the pan and quickly stir fry cabbage, mushrooms and green onions. Add water chestnuts, oyster sauce, sesame oil and the cooked pork. To serve, warm tortillas and spread about 1 teaspoon hoi sin sauce on each. Spread meat mixture down the center of each tortilla and roll up around the filling. Serves 4-6.

*This is available in Oriental grocery stores, or you can substitute 2 cloves of garlic mashed with ⅛ teaspoon of chili pepper flakes.

KONA INN BEEF

2 pounds round steak cut into
   1" cubes
Olive oil
¼ cup sherry
1 10½-ounce can consomme
1 bay leaf
1 clove garlic
1 cup catsup
¼ cup brown sugar
1 tablespoon Worcestershire sauce
1 onion, chopped

¼ cup mushrooms
½ cup raisins
1 tablespoon curry powder
⅛ cup wine
1 - 2 tablespoons cornstarch
½ cup chopped macadamia nuts
½ cup grated coconut
3 tablespoons chopped chives
6 slices bacon, cooked and
   crumbled

Heat olive oil in large skillet and quickly brown the beef cubes. Add sherry, consomme, bay leaf and garlic. Reduce heat and cook slowly for two hours. Add catsup, brown sugar, Worcestershire sauce, wine, onion, raisins, mushrooms and curry powder. Simmer 30 minutes. Mix cornstarch with a little water and add to thicken gravy. Serve over hot rice. Pass separate bowls of macadamia nuts, coconut, chives and bacon as garnish. This recipe does particularly well in a crock pot. Serves 6.

KAL BI

4-5 pounds beef short ribs cut
  Korean style
3-4 cloves garlic, crushed
1 tablespoon sesame seeds,
  toasted and crushed
2 finely chopped green onions

1 teaspoon black pepper
1 teaspoon sesame oil
2 cups shoyu
1 cup sugar
¼ cup oil

Put short ribs in a bowl. Combine all other ingredients and pour over the meat. Toss the ribs in the marinade to coat each rib well. Cover and let stand at room temperature for two hours. Broil over charcoal or under an oven broiler turning and basting with marinade until the meat is just cooked. This will only take a few minutes – watch carefully. Serves 4-6. Several restaurants specialize in these wonderful Korean ribs. The sauce is also delicious with chicken or pork.

OX TAIL STEW

4 pounds of oxtails
Flour
Oil or bacon fat
1 cup water
½ cup sherry
Salt and pepper to taste
2 bay leaves
6 cloves

1 28-ounce can of tomatoes,
   chopped
1 cup chopped onion
2 cloves of garlic, chopped
2 ribs of celery, sliced
2-3 carrots, peeled and sliced
½ pound mushrooms, sliced

Roll oxtails in flour and brown WELL in oil or bacon fat. Pour off fat and add water, sherry, salt, pepper, cloves, bay leaves, and tomatoes. Cover and simmer for two hours. While the meat is cooking, saute onion, celery, garlic and carrots. Add to oxtails and simmer covered for another hour or until they are very tender. Add mushrooms and cook for 15-30 minutes more. In the last few minutes add a little more sherry. This is best made the day ahead and refrigerated. Remove any remaining fat before reheating. Serve with rice. Serves 6.

PARKER RANCH
TERIYAKI STEAK

2-3 pounds round steak
½ cup sugar
⅔ cup shoyu
3 tablespoons sherry
2 tablespoons oil
2 tablespoons toasted sesame seeds

1 stalk green onion, chopped
½ teaspoon salt
1 tablespoon grated ginger
1 clove garlic, crushed
1 tablespoon M.S.G.

Mix ingredients for sauce together and pour over the steak. Let the meat sit in the marinade for several hours and then barbecue, basting occasionally with the rest of the marinade. Serves 4-6.

ITALIAN SANDWICH

4 mild, or sweet, Italian sausages
1 large green pepper seeded and
  cut into 8 strips
1 small onion cut in eighths
½ cup white wine
½ cup water
½ teaspoon oregano

½ teaspoon basil
2 cloves garlic, minced
Loaf of french bread cut in half
  lengthwise
Butter
Blue cheese

Brown sausages in a heavy skillet. Remove and set aside. Saute green pepper strips until slightly limp. Add onions and saute until slightly limp. Add sausages, basil, oregano, garlic, salt and pepper, wine and water. Simmer covered until vegetables are soft, 5-10 minutes. Remove lid and boil down until there is about ½" of liquid in the pan. To serve, warm the french bread and cut into individual servings. Butter both halves. Cut the sausages in half lengthwise and put on bottom halves of the bread. Top with onion and pepper pieces. Dunk the cut side of the top pieces of bread into the sauce in the pan, spread with blue cheese and complete the sandwich. Serves 4-6. This is a dinner to serve to old friends sitting around the kitchen table, or for a family night at home with a movie. It is messy to eat at best, and the chewier the bread the harder the whole sandwich is to deal with — but also the more delicious. We couldn't resist it. Have cold beer and plenty of paper napkins available, and enjoy!

PEKING SESAME BEEF

1 flank steak cut into ½ inch slices
1 tablespoon shoyu
1 tablespoon water
1½ teaspoon white wine
¼ teaspoon baking soda
3 cups oil
3 tablespoons cornstarch
1½ teaspoons chopped green onion
½ teaspoon chopped garlic

½ teaspoon chopped ginger
3 tablespoons water
3 tablespoons shoyu
1 tablespoon sesame oil
1½ teaspoon sugar
Dash of pepper
2 tablespoons sesame seed, toasted
1 pound watercress

Mix 1 tablespoon shoyu, water, wine and soda together. Add the sliced beef and marinate for 1 hour. Heat 3 cups of oil in a wok. Stir 3 tablespoons of cornstarch into beef and mix well. Quickly cook beef strips in the hot oil, 1-2 minutes, remove from oil and drain on absorbant paper. Remove all but 3 tablespoons of oil. Add the chopped green onion, garlic, and ginger and stir fry until fragrant. Add water, shoyu, sesame oil, sugar and pepper. Add the beef and top with the toasted sesame seeds. Cook on high heat until the sauce is almost evaporated. When you are ready to serve, quickly blanch the watercress by plunging into boiling water for one minute. Drain and put on a platter. Top with beef and serve. Serves 4.

UPCOUNTRY STEAK

1½ pounds boneless sirloin
⅓ cup brandy
½ cup brown sauce
⅔ cup whipping cream

1 tablespoon green peppercorns
(or more to taste)
French bread

Heat a heavy frying pan on a burner until very hot. Sprinkle with a fine layer of table salt and add the meat, searing it quickly on both sides. Reduce the heat and continue to cook until the juices begin to seep through the top – or until done to your taste. Remove from pan and keep warm. Pour brandy into the frying pan and, over a medium heat, deglaze the frying pan, scraping up all the brown bits from the bottom and sides of the pan. Add the whipping cream, the brown sauce and the peppercorns, which have been lightly crushed. Simmer for 2-3 minutes until slightly thickened. Put meat on a warm platter and carve in slices, slightly on the diagonal. Cover with the sauce. To serve, put a crouton on the plate and top with 2 or 3 slices of steak with some of the sauce. To prepare croutons: Cut portions of day old bread in approximately the shape of the slices of meat. Using a heavy frying pan saute bread in about 6 tablespoons of clarified butter, turning them until they are golden brown and crisp. Drain on a paper towel and keep warm. Serves 4.

BEEF JERKY

3 pounds round steak, all visible fat removed
1 teaspoon seasoned salt
½ teaspoon garlic powder
½ teaspoon chili powder
¼ cup shoyu
1 tablespoon liquid smoke
½ teaspoon onion powder
¼ cup Worcestershire sauce

Cut round steak into long strips about ⅛″ to ¼″ thick and put in a glass 9″ x 13″ dish. Mix all the other ingredients and pour over the meat, stirring to coat all the pieces with the marinade. Refrigerate for 24 hours. Set the oven at its lowest temperature. Cover the lower rack with aluminum foil. Put the other rack directly above the covered rack and lay the strips of meat on it. Prop the oven door open just a crack and cook for at least 4 hours – 6 if meat is ¼″ thick, or if you like it really dry.

GRILLED LEG OF LAMB

1 leg of lamb, boned and
  butterflied
1 large clove of garlic, split
1½ teaspoon salt
1 teaspoon curry powder

½ teaspoon powdered ginger
¼ teaspoon coarse black pepper
2 tablespoons chutney
⅓ cup fresh lemon juice
⅔ cup salad oil

Rub lamb with the split garlic clove. Mix salt, pepper, ginger and curry and rub into meat. Finely chop chutney and combine with lemon juice and salad oil. Pour over the lamb and marinate several hours or overnight, if possible. Have a medium hot charcoal fire ready. Place lamb fat side up 8-10 inches from the coals. Baste with marinade and cook 20-25 minutes, depending on the thickness of the lamb. Turn meat over and cook for 15 minutes. Lamb will be medium rare. Continue cooking until meat is done to your taste. Serves 6-8.

KONA INN BANANA BREAD

2 cups granulated sugar
1 cup softened butter (not
   margarine)
6 ripe bananas, mashed
   (approximately 3 cups)

4 eggs, well beaten
2½ cups cake flour
2 teaspoons baking soda
1 teaspoon salt

Preheat oven to 350 degrees. With an electric beater cream together sugar
and butter until light and fluffy. Add bananas and eggs, beating until well
mixed. Sift together dry ingredients THREE times and blend with the
banana mixture until JUST blended – don't overmix. Pour into two lightly
greased 5″ x9″ x3″ loaf pans. Bake at 350 degrees for 45 minutes to 1 hour,
until firm in the center and the edges begin to come away from the pan. Cool
on rack for 10 minutes and then remove from the pans. The Kona Inn was
justly famous for its Banana Bread – it is delicious. If you want to enjoy one
loaf immediately and save the other, it will freeze beautifully.

MANGO BREAD

1½ cups butter or oil
2½ cups sugar
6 eggs
2 teaspoons vanilla extract
½ teaspoon coconut extract
4 cups flour

1 teaspoon salt
4 teaspoons baking soda
3 teaspoons cinnamon
4 cups mango puree
1 cup chopped nuts (optional)

Cream butter or oil and sugar. Beat in eggs one at a time. Add vanilla and coconut extract. Sift dry ingredients and add alternately with the mango puree. Pour into three greased 5″ x 9″ x 3″ loaf pans and bake at 350 degrees for 45-55 minutes — or until a toothpick inserted in the center of the loaf comes out clean. Turn loaves out onto a rack and let cool. If you are going to use this for gifts, you might want to use 8 small foil loaf pans (check for doneness at 35 minutes) or a large bundt pan.

POI BISCUITS

1 13-ounce jar poi
⅓ cup flour
1 teaspoon baking powder

½ teaspoon salt
Butter

Sift together flour, baking powder and salt. Add poi and mix well. Roll into balls the size of walnuts. Place on greased cookie sheet and bake at 450 degrees for 20 minutes. Serve immediately with lots of butter. These delectable nuggets have been served as pupus at cocktail parties for as long as any of us can remember. They can also be served with soups and salads, in place of a standard roll with dinner, and of course with a poi supper.

POI NUT BREAD

1 pound poi
¾ cup water
2 cups flour
1 cup sugar
2 teaspoons cinnamon
2 teaspoons baking soda
1 teaspoon salt

3 eggs, slightly beaten
1 cup salad oil
2 teaspoons vanilla
½ cup chopped nuts
½ cup shredded coconut
½ cup raisins

Put poi into a small bowl and add water. Mix well and set aside. Sift dry ingredients together into a large bowl. Take 2 tablespoons of flour and mix with the coconut, raisins and nuts. Set aside. Beat eggs and combine with salad oil and vanilla. Add this to the flour mixture. Add poi and mix well. Fold in coconut, raisins and nuts. Pour into two 5 x 9 inch loaf pans, well greased, and bake at 350 degrees for 45 minutes. This is a heavy, moist and delicious bread — slightly pink in color and extremely nourishing, because of the poi, but it has only a hint of taro flavor.

ZELIE'S OATMEAL MUFFINS

1 cup regular rolled oats
1 cup buttermilk
1 egg, well beaten
½ cup brown sugar
1 cup flour

1 teaspoon baking powder
½ teaspoon baking soda
1 teaspoon salt
½ cup oil

Soak rolled oats in buttermilk for one hour. Beat egg and add sugar. Add to softened oats and buttermilk. Sift together flour, baking powder, salt and baking soda. Mix into the oat mixture. Stir in oil and mix well. Spoon into 12 oiled muffin cups, filling each about ⅔ full. Bake in oven preheated to 400 degrees for 20-25 minutes. This muffin freezes well and the recipe can be doubled, tripled or quadrupled successfully. You can find a recipe for oatmeal muffins in any basic cookbook but for some reason, whenever these particular muffins are served, everyone wants the recipe.

CHUTNEY BREAD

2½ cups flour
½ cup granulated sugar
½ cup brown sugar, packed
1 teaspoon baking powder
1 teaspoon salt
3 tablespoons oil

1¼ cup milk
1 egg
1 tablespoon orange peel
1 10-ounce jar mild chutney, chopped
1 cup chopped nuts

Combine flour, sugars, baking powder, salt, oil, milk, egg and orange peel. Mix just enough to moisten ingredients. Do not overmix. Fold in the chutney and the nuts. Turn into a greased 5" x 9" x 3" loaf pan and bake at 350 degrees 55-60 minutes, or until golden brown on top and the cake tester comes out clean. Bread will be moist. Mango chutney is such an island treat that we couldn't resist adding this recipe — even though it is generally more appealing to ladies than to men. It is wonderful served with a papaya half filled with curried chicken salad.

HIXON'S COCONUT BREAD

4½ cups unbleached flour
3 teaspoons baking powder
1 teaspoon salt
1½ cups raw or light brown sugar
3 cups grated coconut, unsweetened
1 teaspoon baking soda
1 cup buttermilk

1½ teaspoons vanilla
¾ cup butter or margarine, melted
3 eggs, well beaten
¼ teaspoon almond extract
1 cup evaporated milk
¼ cup granulated sugar for top

Sift flour, baking powder and salt; mix with sugar and coconut. Dissolve soda in buttermilk. Beat together butter, eggs, vanilla and almond extract. Add evaporated milk. Stir into the flour mixture and mix lightly but thoroughly. Pour into two greased loaf pans, 4"x8". Sprinkle the tops with sugar. Bake at 350 degrees for 55 minutes, or until toothpick inserted in the center comes out clean. Partially cool in pan and then turn out onto a rack to complete the cooling.

GLORIA'S TENDER ROLLS

1 tablespoon active dry yeast
1¼ cup lukewarm milk
1 teaspoon salt
½ cup oil

3 tablespoons honey
3 well beaten eggs
4¼ cups whole wheat flour
(more if you need it)

Soften yeast in milk. Add salt, oil, honey and eggs. Slowly beat in flour. When dough gets too stiff, turn out on a floured board and knead in the rest — and more if you need it. Continue to knead until the dough is elastic (about 10 minutes). Put into an oiled bowl, lightly oil the top of the dough, cover with saran wrap and a towel and let sit in a warm place for 1½ hours to rise. Punch the dough down and let rise again — this time for 45 minutes. Pat dough out into a circle 12″ in diameter and brush with melted butter. Cut circle into 16 pie shaped pieces and roll each to form a butterhorn (begin at the wide end and roll toward the tip.) Place rolls on two well greased cookie sheets and let rise to double their original size. Bake about 15 minutes in an oven preheated to 400 degrees.

PORTUGUESE SWEET BREAD

1 package active dry yeast
¼ cup warm water
¼ cup butter
¼ cup hot water
¾ cup plus 1⅓ tablespoon
   evaporated milk

⅝ cup sugar
3 eggs, well beaten
1½ teaspoon vanilla
4 cups plus 1 tablespoon flour

Dissolve yeast in warm water. Melt butter in hot water. Add milk to butter and water mixture. Beat eggs and sugar together, add vanilla, milk, butter, water and yeast to the flour. Mix well and turn out onto a lightly floured board. Knead for at least 15 minutes. Put into an oiled bowl, cover with plastic wrap and a clean towel. Put in a warm, draft free place to rise for 1½ hours. Punch down and shape into 3 round loaves. Place each in a greased 9" cake pan. Cover as before and allow to rise again for 1 hour. Bake for 30 to 40 minutes at 325 degrees. When the loaves come out of the oven, immediately run a cube of butter over the top. In the "old days" there was a large Portuguese community in up-country Maui which used to make this wonderful bread in bee-hive shaped stone ovens, heated with kiawe wood fires. A modern oven is acceptable however, and does produce a memorable treat.

OATMEAL PANCAKES

2 cups regular rolled oats
2 cups buttermilk
2 eggs, lightly beaten
¼ cup butter, melted and cooled
½ cups raisins
½ cup flour

2 tablespoons sugar
1 teaspoon baking powder
1 teaspoon baking soda
½ teaspoon ground cinnamon
¼ teaspoon salt

In a bowl combine oats and buttermilk and stir to blend well. Cover and chill overnight. In the morning add the eggs, butter and raisins. Stir to blend. In another bowl combine the flour, sugar, baking powder, soda, cinnamon and salt. Add to the oat mixture and stir just until moistened. If batter seems too thick, stir in up to 3 tablespoons more buttermilk. Cook on well greased griddle over medium heat. These pancakes take a bit longer to cook than usual. Makes about 18 pancakes.

COCONUT POUND CAKE

1 cup butter, softened
½ cup vegetable shortening
3 cups sugar
6 eggs
1 teaspoon lemon juice
1 teaspoon vanilla

1 teaspoon almond flavoring
1 teaspoon coconut flavoring
3 cups flour
1 cup milk
1 3½-ounce can flaked coconut

Preheat oven to 325 degrees. Cream butter, sugar and shortening. Add eggs one at a time, beating after each addition. Add flavoring and remaining ingredients, alternating flour and milk, about one third at a time. Fold in coconut. Bake in a greased tube pan for about 1½ hours. This cake keeps forever in the refrigerator. It also freezes beautifully.

ORANGE POUND CAKE

1 cup margarine
2 cups sugar
5 eggs
3 cups sifted flour
3 teaspoons baking powder
¼ teaspoon salt
¾ cup orange juice (must be
  fresh, not frozen)
Grated rind of 1 orange

Glaze:
¼ cup margarine
⅓ cup bourbon
⅔ cup sugar

Cream margarine and sugar until fluffy. Beat in eggs one at a time. Sift dry ingredients and add to batter alternately with orange juice, ending with orange juice. Add grated rind. Pour into a greased and floured tube pan. Bake at 350 degrees for 1 hour. Remove cake from the oven, put the ingredients for the glaze in a saucepan and heat until the sugar is dissolved. DO NOT LET BOIL. Prick the top of the cake with a fork and then pour glaze evenly over the cake. Leave in the pan until thoroughly cooled. This cake can be made ahead and frozen, or kept in the refrigerator until ready to serve.

LYCHEE GINGER SAUCE

1 jar ginger preserves
2 tablespoons orange juice
1 tablespoon fresh lemon or
   lime juice

1 tablespoon Cointreau
1 15-ounce can lychees
1 quart vanilla ice cream

Put ginger preserves, orange juice, lemon or lime juice into a blender and blend until the pieces of ginger are quite small. Taste and add more Cointreau if needed. Drain lychees and cut in half. Arrange halves around scoops of ice cream and pour several tablespoons of syrup over each serving.

HOT FUDGE SAUCE

4 ounces unsweetened chocolate
½ cup butter
⅓ cup unsweetened cocoa
1½ cup sugar
1 cup whipping cream

Melt chocolate in a double boiler. Add butter, cocoa and sugar. Cook about 30-40 minutes. Add cream and cook 5 to 10 minutes longer, stirring constantly. Slowly add the flavoring of your choice. Makes 3 cups. Can be stored in the refrigerator up to three weeks — if you are able to keep it that long! Choice of flavoring might include 1 teaspoon of vanilla, rum or mint extract, or 2 tablespoons of peanut butter.

VANILLA SAUCE

1 cup confectioners sugar
3 tablespoons butter, melted
1 egg yolk

¼ teaspoon vanilla
⅛ teaspoon salt
1 cup heavy cream

Beat sugar, butter, egg yolk, vanilla and salt together. In a separate bowl beat heavy cream until soft peaks form. Fold the whipped cream into the sugar mixture. It will make a lovely sauce which is more stable than whipped cream and is particularly good on a hot souffle or pudding.

GINGER SOUFFLE

3 tablespoons butter
3 tablespoons flour
1 cup milk
⅓ cup sugar
⅛ teaspoon salt
1 tablespoon cognac

1 teaspoon powdered ginger
½ cup drained preserved or
    crystallized ginger, finely
    chopped or ground
4 eggs, separated

Preheat oven to 375 degrees. Butter a 2-quart casserole and sprinkle the sides and bottom generously with granulated sugar. Set aside. Melt butter in a saucepan and add flour, stirring until blended. In another saucepan scald the milk. Add milk all at once to the flour and butter mixture, and stir well with a wire whisk until mixture thickens. Add the sugar, salt, cognac and ginger. Remove from the stove. Beat egg yolks, one at a time, into the mixture. Cool. Beat egg whites until they stand in peaks and fold into the cooled mixture. Pour gently into casserole and bake from 35-45 minutes. Serve immediately. Pass a bowl of creme fraiche or whipped cream if desired.

HORATIO'S BURNT CREME

2 cups whipping cream
4 egg yolks
½ cup granulated sugar
1 tablespoon vanilla

Preheat oven to 350 degrees. Heat cream over low heat until bubbles form around edge of the pan. Beat egg yolks and sugar together until thick, about 3 minutes. Gradually beat cream into the egg yolks. Stir in vanilla. Pour into six 6-ounce individual souffle dishes, or similar size oven-proof, shallow dessert containers. Place containers in baking pan that has about ½ inch water in the bottom. Bake for approximately 45 minutes, or until set. Remove from water and refrigerate until well chilled. Sprinkle each serving with about two teaspoons granulated sugar. Preheat broiler. Place containers on a tray and slip the whole tray quickly under the broiler and cook until topping is medium brown. Watch carefully. Chill again before serving.

Horatio's Restaurant in Honolulu is famous for this marvelous, rich dessert.

STRAWBERRIES BRULEE

6 cups strawberries, washed
  and hulled
¼ cup Grand Marnier
2 cups milk

½ cup Wondra flour
4 egg yolks
1 cup whipping cream
1 cup light brown sugar

Prepare strawberries. Put them in an even layer on a platter or in a shallow casserole that can go into the oven. Sprinkle the Grand Marnier over the berries. Scald milk and using a whisk SLOWLY add the flour. You must use Wondra flour or this will not work. Beat egg yolks together and add to flour mixture, mixing well. Remove from heat and cool with plastic wrap on the surface to prevent skin from forming on the top. When this mixture is cold, whip the cream and fold into the pudding. Gently spread over the berries in an even blanket, going all the way out to the edge all around. No berries should be showing, ideally, nor should there be mounds of berries sticking up. Sift the brown sugar all over the top in another nice even layer. Preheat broiler and when hot, run the platter underneath and cook just long enough to melt the brown sugar. You may want to use more or less brown sugar, depending on the size container you use, and your taste. This is an unusual and delicious dessert. Do try it when strawberries are in season.

PUMPKIN SQUARES

1 29-ounce can pumpkin pie mix
1 5-ounce can evaporated milk
3 eggs, lightly beaten
1 cup sugar
½ teaspoon salt
2 teaspoon cinnamon

1 package yellow cake mix
  with pudding
½ pound butter, melted and
  cooled slightly
1 cup chopped nuts

Preheat oven to 350 degrees. Line a 9″ x 14″ pan with waxed paper. Mix together the pumpkin, milk, sugar, eggs, salt and cinnamon. Pour into pan. Sprinkle cake mix over the top. Distribute chopped nuts over cake mix and drizzle melted butter over all. Bake 1¼ hours. Chill. Invert and cut into bars. Small bars can be eaten in the fingers. Large bars or squares can be served on a plate, topped with a dollop of whipped cream. This is a delicious alternative to pumpkin pie and extremely easy to make. Do not be thrown off by the use of the packaged cake mix.

SHERRY CREAM PIE

1 envelope unflavored gelatin
¼ cup milk
½ cup sugar
1 cup milk
⅛ teaspoon nutmeg

½ cup dry sherry
1 cup heavy cream
Crust:
20 Oreo cookies
2 tablespoons melted butter

Separate eggs, placing yolks in double broiler top, whites in a small bowl. Sprinkle gelatin over ¼ cup milk and let stand 5 minutes. Beat egg yolks and stir in sugar and 1 cup milk. Cook over hot water until thickened, about 10 minutes. Add softened gelatin, salt and nutmeg. Stir until dissolved. Slowly add sherry. Refrigerate until mixture just begins to thicken. Beat egg whites and cream, separately, until peaks form. Gently fold whipped cream and the custard mixture into the egg whites. Mix together quickly but well. Pour into pie crust and refrigerate. Decorate top with chopped macadamia nuts or shaved chocolate. Chill overnight. For crust: Crush 20 Oreo cookies and mix with 2 tablespoons melted butter. Press into a 10" pie pan.

MANGO CREAM

1½ teaspoons unflavored gelatin
4 tablespoons water
½ cup water
Dash of salt
1 cup mango puree (fresh is much
    better than frozen)

3 tablespoons lime juice (fresh
    if possible)
⅓ cup of sugar
½ cups heavy cream, whipped

Sprinkle gelatin over 4 tablespoons water and let stand for five minutes. Put ½ cup water and dash of salt in a pan and bring to a boil. Add sugar and stir to dissolve. Remove from heat and add the softened gelatin. Stir until dissolved and cool. Add mango puree and lime juice. Blend well and chill. When mixture is beginning to set, and has the consistency of raw egg whites, whip the cream and gently fold into the mango mixture. Refrigerate for at least four hours. This is a light and lovely dessert. Pour it into your best glass bowl, decorate the top with whipped cream and a few candied violets and you will have an elegant finale to your dinner with very little time or effort.

SLICED LEMON PIE

2 whole lemons, thinly sliced
2 cups sugar
4 eggs, well beaten
1 unbaked pie shell

3 cups sifted flour
1 cup shortening
1 egg
1 tablespoon vinegar
2-3 tablespoons water

Slice lemons as thinly as possible (do not peel). Discard seeds and combine lemon slices with sugar and allow to stand while making the pastry. Cut 1 cup of shortening into 3 cups sifted flour until the mixture has the consistency of cornmeal. Add 1 whole egg and 1 tablespoon vinegar. Mix well and add 2-3 tablespoons of water, 1 tablespoon at a time, working in with a fork until the mixture leaves the side of the bowl. Divide dough in half. Roll out half and fit into the pie pan. Roll out the other half and cut into strips for the lattice top. Set aside. Beat eggs well and stir into the lemon mixture. Pour into the shell, cover with lattice and bake at 450 degrees for 10 minutes. Reduce heat to 350 degrees and bake 35 minutes longer.

FROZEN CHOCOLATE PIE

Crust:
2 cups finely chopped pecans,
  toasted
⅓ cup firmly packed brown sugar
5 tablespoons butter
2 teaspoons dark rum

Filling:
6-ounces semi-sweet chocolate
1 teaspoon vanilla
½ teaspoon instant coffee powder
4 eggs
1 tablespoon dark rum
1½ cups whipping cream
3 tablespoons shaved semi-sweet
  chocolate

Blend all the crust ingredients in a bowl. Lightly butter a 10″ springform pan. Press mixture into pan and part way up the sides. Chill in freezer for one hour. While crust is chilling, prepare the following filling. Melt chocolate in double broiler. Remove and beat in eggs one at a time. Add rum, coffee and vanilla. Cool 5 minutes. Whip one cup of cream until stiff. Gently fold into chocolate mixture. Pour into crust and return to the freezer. One hour before serving, put pie in the refrigerator. Decorate with remaining cream, whipped, and shaved chocolate. Serves 12.

COCONUT PIE

1 9" unbaked pie shell
1 egg
1 cup milk
1 cup sugar

1 teaspoon vanilla
Pinch of salt
2 3½-ounce cans grated coconut
2 tablespoons melted butter

Prepare the pie shell by mixing together 1½ cups flour, ½ teaspoon salt, and ½ teaspoon sugar. Cut in ¼ cup butter. Add ¼ cup oil and mix well. Add 3 tablespoons of water, a tablespoon at a time, mixing well after each addition, until the dough leaves the sides of the bowl and forms a ball. Roll out and fit into a 9" pie pan. Mix the egg, milk, sugar, vanilla and salt with an electric mixer. Pour into pie crust and pat in one or more cups of grated coconut. Top with 2 tablespoons melted butter. Bake at 300 degrees for 40-50 minutes.

FRESH PINEAPPLE COBBLER

4 cups pineapple chunks
1 cup sugar
⅓ cup pancake mix (or Bisquick)
1 teaspoon grated lemon peel

¾ cup pancake mix (or Bisquick)
⅔ cup sugar
1 beaten egg
¼ cup butter

Combine first four ingredients and pour into a 9″ square pan. Combine next three ingredients and spread over pineapple mixture. Melt butter and drizzle over the top. Bake 35-40 minutes at 350 degrees. Serve warm with whipped cream or ice cream.

PINEAPPLE CHEESE BAKLAVA

1 20-ounce can crushed pineapple
   in syrup
1 8-ounce package cream cheese,
   softened
1 cup ricotta cheese
1 cup sugar
2 egg yolks

1 tablespoon grated lemon peel
1 teaspoon vanilla
½ pound frozen phyllo pastry
   leaves, thawed (8 leaves)
½ cup butter, melted
1 teaspoon lemon juice

Drain pineapple well and save the juice. In a medium size mixing bowl combine cream cheese, ricotta cheese, ½ cup sugar, egg yolks, lemon peel, vanilla and blend with an electric mixer on medium speed. Stir in drained pineapple. Place phyllo leaves on plastic wrap between moist towels. Place one sheet of pastry in well greased 9" x 13" x 2" pan. Brush with melted butter. Repeat with three more leaves. Spoon on the pineapple-cheese mix and spread level. Top with remaining phyllo, brushing each sheet with butter as it is layered. Mark pastry into diamonds with sharp knife point. Bake at 350 degrees for about 50 minutes or until golden brown. Combine ½ cup reserved pineapple juice, remaining sugar and lemon juice. Cook to a thick syrup. Spoon the hot syrup evenly over the top of the baklava. Cool and cut into diamonds at the markings. Serves 8. This recipe was the winner of the Pineapple Cooking Classic, a cooking contest which was held annually in Honolulu.

THE WILLOWS SKY HIGH
COCONUT CREAM PIE

1 9″ pie crust, baked
2 cups milk
1 tablespoon butter
½ cup sugar
¼ cup grated coconut
4 egg yolks
Pinch of salt
2 heaping tablespoons cornstarch

¼ teaspoon vanilla
6 egg whites
½ teaspoon salt
½ teaspoon cream of tartar
6 tablespoon sugar
½ teaspoon vanilla
Grated coconut for top

Sift together 1½ cups flour, ½ teaspoon salt and ½ teaspoon sugar. Cut in ¼ cup butter, then add ¼ cup oil and mix well. Add 3 tablespoons cold water, 1 tablespoon at a time, mixing well after each addition. Stir until dough leaves the sides of the bowl and forms a ball. Roll out and fit into a 9″ pie pan. Prick bottom and sides and bake at 425 degrees until lightly browned. Cool. In a saucepan combine milk, butter, sugar, coconut and salt. Let come to a near boil. Mix egg yolks, cornstarch and vanilla together and add to the milk mixture. Let cook for a few minutes, stirring constantly until mixture thickens. Remove from heat and put a sheet of plastic wrap over the top to keep crust from forming on the pudding and allow it to cool. Fill the pastry shell with the coconut pudding and top with meringue made by beating the egg whites, salt, and cream of tartar until the whites are stiff but not dry. Slowly add sugar, continuing to beat. Stir in vanilla. Spread meringue on pie filling, sealing to the edges of the pastry. Sprinkle coconut over the top and brown in a 400 degree oven. The Willows Restaurant in Honolulu has served this impressive pie as one of their specialties for over thirty years – to the delight of local residents and visitors alike. The fresher the ingredients the better the pie. The use of fresh coconut really makes it special, but you can substitute canned coconut flakes, or frozen grated coconut.

TROPICAL TRIFLE

2 pound cakes, 10¾-ounces each
18-24 coconut cookies, crumbled
1½ cups medium sweet sherry
6 tablespoons brandy
1 18-ounce jar guava jelly
1 18-ounce jar pineapple preserve
2½ cups thick pastry cream, cooled

2 tablespoons finely chopped
    crystallized ginger
1 cup whipping cream
1 tablespoon sifted confectioners
    sugar
1 teaspoon sherry
½ cup chopped macadamia nuts

In a deep dish or bowl, clear glass preferably, layer half the pound cake and half the crumbled cookies. Sprinkle with ¾ cup sherry and 3 tablespoons brandy. Let soak 15 minutes. Spread thickly with guava jelly. Gently mix the chopped ginger into the pastry cream and spread half the mixture over the guava jelly. Add another layer of cake and crumbled cookies. Sprinkle with the remaining sherry and brandy. Top with the pineapple preserve and the remaining pastry cream. Cover with plastic wrap and refrigerate until ready to serve. Just before serving whip cream until it thickens. Add confectioners sugar and sherry and continue whipping until soft peaks form. Cover the trifle with whipped cream and sprinkle with macadamia nuts. Serve immediately. Serves 16.

TROPICAL TRIFLE PASTRY CREAM

6 egg yolks
½ cup granulated sugar
½ cup flour

2 cups hot milk
2 tablespoons butter
1 tablespoon vanilla

Put egg yolks in a heavy saucepan. Add sugar and beat until mixture is thick and forms ribbons when the beater is lifted from it. Beat in flour and then slowly beat in the hot milk. Cook over medium heat, stirring with a whisk constantly until the mixture thickens. Reduce heat a little and beat vigorously to keep mixture smooth as it thickens. Remove from heat and add butter and vanilla. Cover top with plastic film and refrigerate until ready to use. This can be made the day before, if you wish.

CREDITS

(Photo from left to right: Dot Russell, Zelie Harders, Carol Hartley, and Judy Bisgard.)

Maui Cooks was conceived for the purpose of raising funds to support the Maui Kokua Services, a United Way agency. In Hawaiian the word "kokua" means "helping." This agency was established in 1980 to provide a link between individuals who have a need for services and those who have a service to offer the community.

(Photo from left to right: Gini Baldwin, Penny James, Hilary Parker, Heather Cole, and Judy Furtado.)

The nine women who participated in this project are known for their love of cooking and entertaining. Of the nine cooks, Heather Cole, Judy Bisgard, and Zelie Harders were born and raised in Hawaii and from their recipe files come many "old style" family treasures. Penny James added her experience working on the Seabury Hall cookbook. Judy Furtado brought 15 years of restaurant experience in Hawaii. Dot Russell, Hilary Parker, Gini Baldwin and Carol Hartley drew from living on Maui since before statehood. This cookbook is brought to you after three years of these cooks meeting in Gini's Kula kitchen to cook, taste, test and select the recipes.

(Photo from left to right: Kaui Goring, Darrell Orwig, and Jill Weed.)

Darrell Orwig, an established local artist, rendered the original oil pastels of small local Maui markets while Kaui Goring, Food Editor and Feature Writer for The Maui News, wrote the narrative. Jill Weed designed and compiled this work to bring Maui Cooks to you.

Mahalo! A special thank you to Lloyd Komoda and Lori Mooney at Ace Printing, to Randy Hufford at Maui Custom Color, to Susan Vanderhorst, to LaVonne Tollerud of Creative Cookery, to our families, and finally, our friends.

INDEX

144

This book is available by mail for $13.95 which includes postage and handling. Please write: Maui Cooks Inc., 461 Aulii Drive, Pukalani, Maui, Hawaii 96788.